The fixed period : a novel Volume 1 – Primary Source Edition

Trollope, Anthony, 1815-1882

THE FIXED PERIOD

ORIGINALLY PUBLISHED IN 'BLACKWOOD'S MAGAZINE'

THE FIXED PERIOD

A NOVEL

BY

ANTHONY TROLLOPE

IN TWO VOLUMES

VOL. I.

WILLIAM BLACKWOOD AND SONS
EDINBURGH AND LONDON
MDCCCLXXXII

CONTENTS OF VOL. I.

	PAGE
. INTRODUCTION, ...	1
. GABRIEL CRASWELLER, ...	27
. THE FIRST BREAK-DOWN, . . .	55
. JACK NEVERBEND, ...	86
. THE CRICKET-MATCH, . . .	123
. THE COLLEGE, ...	169

THE FIXED PERIOD.

——◆——

CHAPTER I.

INTRODUCTION.

It may be doubted whether a brighter, more prosperous, and specially a more orderly colony than Britannula was ever settled by British colonists. But it had its period of separation from the mother country, though never of rebellion,—like its elder sister New Zealand. Indeed, in that respect it simply followed the lead given her by the Australias, which, when they set up for themselves, did so with the full co-operation of England. There was, no doubt, a special cause with us which did not exist in Australia, and which was only, in part, understood by the British Government when we Britannulists were allowed to stand by ourselves. The great doctrine of a "Fixed Period" was received by them at first with ridicule, and then with dismay; but it was undoubtedly the strong faith which we of Britannula had in that doctrine which induced our separation. Nothing could have been more successful than our efforts to live alone during the thirty years that we remained our own masters. We repudiated no debt,— as have done some of our neighbours; and no attempts have been made towards communism, —as has been the case with others. We have been laborious, contented, and prosperous; and if we have been reabsorbed by the mother country, in accordance with what I cannot but call the pusillanimous conduct of certain of our elder Britannulists, it has not been from any failure on the part of the island, but from the opposition with which the Fixed Period has been regarded.

I think I must begin my story by explaining in moderate language a few of the manifest advantages which would attend the adoption of the Fixed Period in all countries. As far as the law went it was adopted in Britannula. Its adoption was the first thing discussed by our young Assembly, when we found ourselves alone; and though there were disputes on the subject, in none of them was opposition made to the system. I myself, at the age of thirty, had been elected Speaker of that Parliament. But I was, nevertheless, able to discuss the merits of the bills in committee, and I did so with some enthusiasm. Thirty years have passed since, and my "period" is drawing nigh. But I am still as energetic as ever, and as assured that the doctrine will ultimately prevail over the face of the civilised world, though I will acknowledge that men are not as yet ripe for it.

The Fixed Period has been so far discussed as to make it almost unnecessary for me to explain its tenets, though its advantages may require a few words of argument in a world that is at present dead to its charms. It consists altogether of the abolition of the miseries, weakness, and *fainéant* imbecility of old age, by the prearranged ceasing to live of those who would otherwise become old. Need I explain to the inhabitants of England, for whom I chiefly write, how extreme are those sufferings, and how great the costliness of that old age which is unable in any degree to supply its own wants? Such old age should not, we Britannulists maintain, be allowed to be. This should be prevented, in the interests both of the young and of those who do become old when obliged to linger on after their " period " of work is over. Two mistakes have been made by mankind in reference to their own race,—first, in allowing the world to be burdened with the continued maintenance of those whose cares should have been made to cease, and whose troubles should be at an end. Does not the Psalmist say the same?—" If by reason of strength they be fourscore years, yet is their strength labour and sorrow." And the second, in requiring those who remain to live a useless and painful life. Both these errors have come from an ill-judged and a thoughtless tenderness,—a tenderness to the young in not calling upon them to provide for the decent and comfortable departure of their progenitors ; and a tenderness to the old lest the man, when uninstructed and unconscious of good and evil, should be unwilling to leave the world for which he is not fitted. But such tenderness is no better than unpardonable weakness. Statistics have told us that the sufficient sustenance of an old man is more costly than the feeding of a young one,—as is also the care, nourishment, and education of the as yet unprofitable child. Statistics also have told us that the unprofitable young and the no less unprofitable old form a third of the population. Let the reader think of the burden with which the labour of the world is thus saddled. To these are to be added all who, because of illness cannot work, and because of idleness will not. How are a people to thrive when so weighted? And for what good? As for the children, they are clearly necessary. They have to be nourished in order that they may do good work as their time shall come. But for whose good are the old and effete to be maintained amid all these troubles and miseries? Had there been any one in our Parliament capable of showing that they could reasonably desire it, the bill would not have been passed. Though to me the politico - economical view of the subject was always very strong, the relief to be brought to the aged was the one argument to which no reply could be given.

It was put forward by some who opposed the movement, that the old themselves would not like it. I never felt sure of that, nor do I now. When the colony had become used to the Fixed Period system, the old would become accustomed as well as the young. It is to be understood that a euthanasia was to be prepared for them;—and how many, as men now are, does a euthanasia await? And they would depart with the full respect of all their fellow-citizens. To how many does that lot now fall? During the last years of their lives they were to be saved from any of the horrors of poverty. How many now lack the comforts they cannot earn for themselves? And to them there would be no degraded feeling that they were the recipients of charity. They would be prepared for their departure, for the benefit of their country, surrounded by all the comforts to which, at their time of life, they would be susceptible, in a college maintained at the public expense; and each, as he drew nearer to the happy day, would be treated with still increasing honour. I myself had gone most closely into the question of expense, and had found that by the use of machinery the college could almost be made self-supporting. But we should save on an average £50 for each man and woman who had departed. When our population should have become a million, presuming that one only in fifty would have reached the desired age, the sum actually saved to the colony would amount to £1,000,000 a-year. It would keep us out of debt, make for us our railways, render all our rivers navigable, construct our bridges, and leave us shortly the richest people on God's earth! And this would be effected by a measure doing more good to the aged than to any other class of the community!

Many arguments were used against us, but were vain and futile in their conception. In it religion was brought to bear; and in talking of this the terrible word "murder" was brought into common use. I remember startling the House by forbidding any member to use a phrase so revolting to the majesty of the people. Murder! Did any one who attempted to deter us by the use of foul language, bethink himself that murder, to be murder, must be opposed to the law? This thing was to be done by the law. There can be no other murder. If a murderer be hanged, —in England, I mean, for in Britannula we have no capital punishment,—is that murder? It is not so, only because the law enacts it. I and a few others did succeed at last in stopping the use of that word. Then they talked to us of Methuselah, and endeavoured to draw an argument from the age of the patriarchs. I asked them in committee whether they were prepared to prove that the 969 years, as spoken of in Genesis, were the same measure of time as 969 years now, and told them that if the sanitary arrangements of the world would again permit men to live as long as the patriarchs, we would gladly change the Fixed Period.

In fact, there was not a word to be said against us except that which referred to the feelings of the young and old. Feelings are changeable, I told them at that great and glorious meeting which we had at Gladstonopolis, and though naturally governed only by instinct, would be taught at last to comply with reason. I had lately read how feelings had been allowed in England to stand in the way of the great work of cremation. A son will not like, you say, to lead his father into the college. But ought he not to like to do so? and if so, will not reason teach him to like to do what he ought? I can conceive with rapture the pride, the honour, the affection with which, when the Fixed Period had come, I could have led my father into the college, there to enjoy for twelve months that preparation for euthanasia which no cares for this world would be allowed to disturb. All the existing ideas of the grave would be absent. There would be no further struggles to prolong the time of misery which nature had herself produced. That temptation to the young to begrudge to the old the costly comforts which they could not earn would be no longer fostered. It would be a pride for the young man to feel that his parent's name had been enrolled to all coming time in the bright books of the college which was to be established for the Fixed Period. I have a son of my own, and I have carefully educated him to look forward to the day in which he shall deposit me there as the proudest of his life. Circumstances, as I shall relate in this story, have somewhat interfered with him; but he will, I trust, yet come back to the right way of thinking. That I shall never spend that last happy year within the walls of the college, is to me, from a selfish point of view, the saddest part of England's re-assuming our island as a colony.

My readers will perceive that I am an enthusiast. But there are reforms so great that a man cannot but be enthusiastic when he has received into his very soul the truth of any human improvement. Alas me! I shall never

live to see carried out the glory of this measure
to which I have devoted the best years of my
existence. The college, which has been built
under my auspices as a preparation for the
happy departure, is to be made a Chamber of
Commerce. Those aged men who were awaiting, as I verily believe, in impatience the coming day of their perfected dignity, have been
turned loose in the world, and allowed to grovel
again with mundane thoughts amidst the idleness of years that are useless. Our bridges,
our railways, our Government are not provided
for. Our young men are again becoming torpid
beneath the weight imposed upon them. I
was, in truth, wrong to think that so great a
reform could be brought to perfection within
the days of the first reformers. A divine idea
has to be made common to men's minds by fre-
quent ventilation before it will be seen to be
fit for humanity. Did not the first Christians
all suffer affliction, poverty, and martyrdom?
How many centuries has it taken in the his-

tory of the world to induce it to denounce the not yet abolished theory of slavery? A throne, a lord, and a bishop still remain to encumber the earth! What right had I, then, as the first of the Fixed-Periodists, to hope that I might live to see my scheme carried out, or that I might be allowed to depart as among the first glorious recipients of its advantages?

It would appear absurd to say that had there been such a law in force in England, England would not have prevented its adoption in Britannula. That is a matter of course. But it has been because the old men are still alive in England that the young in Britannula are to be afflicted,—the young and the old as well. The Prime Minister in Downing Street was seventy-two when we were debarred from carrying out our project, and the Secretary for the Colonies was sixty-nine. Had they been among us, and had we been allowed to use our wisdom without interference from effete old age, where would they have been? I wish to speak with all respect of Sir William Gladstone. When we named our metropolis after him, we were aware of his good qualities. He has not the eloquence of his great-grandfather, but he is, they tell us, a safe man. As to the Minister for the Crown Colonies,—of which, alas! Britannula has again become one,—I do not, I own, look upon him as a great statesman. The present Duke of Hatfield has none of the dash, if he has more than the prudence, of his grandfather. He was elected to the present Upper Chamber as a strong anti-Church Liberal, but he never has had the spirit to be a true reformer. It is now due to the "feelings" which fill no doubt the bosoms of these two anti-Fixed-Period seniors, that the doctrine of the Fixed Period has for a time been quenched in Britannula. It is sad to think that the strength and intellect and spirit of manhood should thus be conquered by that very imbecility which it is their desire to banish from the world.

Two years since I had become the President

of that which we gloried to call the rising
Empire of the South Pacific. And in spite of
all internal opposition, the college of the Fixed
Period was already completed. I then received
violent notice from the British Government
that Britannula had ceased to be independent,
and had again been absorbed by the mother
country among the Crown Colonies. How that
information was received, and with what weakness on the part of the Britannulists, I now
proceed to tell.

I confess that I for one was not at first prepared to obey. We were small, but we were
independent, and owed no more of submission
to Great Britain than we do to the Salomon
Islands or to Otaheite. It was for us to make
our own laws, and we had hitherto made them
in conformity with the institutions, and, I
must say, with the prejudices of so-called civilisation. We had now made a first attempt
at progress beyond these limits, and we were
immediately stopped by the fatuous darkness

of the old men whom, had Great Britain
known her own interest, she would already
have silenced by a Fixed Period law on her
own account. No greater instance of uncalled-
for tyranny is told of in the history of the
world as already written. But my brother
Britannulists did not agree with me that, in
the interest of the coming races, it was our
duty rather to die at our posts than yield to
the menaces of the Duke of Hatfield. One
British gunboat, they declared, in the harbour
of Gladstonopolis, would reduce us—to order.
What order? A 250-ton steam-swiveller
could no doubt crush us, and bring our Fixed
Period college in premature ruin about our
ears. But, as was said, the captain of the
gunboat would never dare to touch the wire
that should commit so wide a destruction. An
Englishman would hesitate to fire a shot that
would send perhaps five thousand of his fellow-creatures to destruction before their Fixed
Period. But even in Britannula fear still

remains. It was decided, I will confess by the common voice of the island, that we should admit this Governor, and swear fealty again to the British Crown. Sir Ferdinando Brown was allowed to land, and by the rejoicing made at the first Government House ball, as I have already learned since I left the island, it appeared that the Britannulists rejoiced rather than otherwise at their thraldom.

Two months have passed since that time, and I, being a worn-out old man, and fitted only for the glory of the college, have nothing left me but to write this story, so that coming ages may see how noble were our efforts. But in truth, the difficulties which lay in our way were very stern. The philosophical truth on which the system is founded was too strong, too mighty, too divine, to be adopted by man in the immediate age of its first appearance. But it has appeared; and I perhaps should be contented and gratified, during the years which I am doomed to linger through impotent im-

becility, to think that I have been the first
reformer of my time, though I shall be doomed
to perish without having enjoyed its fruits.

I must now explain before I begin my story
certain details of our plan, which created much
schism among ourselves. In the first place,
what should be the Fixed Period? When a
party of us, three or four hundred in number,
first emigrated from New Zealand to Britannula, we were, almost all of us, young people.
We would not consent to measures in regard
to their public debt which the Houses in
New Zealand threatened to take; and as this
island had been discovered, and a part of it
cultivated, thither we determined to go. Our
resolution was very popular, not only with
certain parties in New Zealand, but also in
the mother country. Others followed us, and
we settled ourselves with great prosperity.
But we were essentially a young community.
There were not above ten among us who had
then reached any Fixed Period; and not above

twenty others who could be said to be approaching it. There never could arrive a time or a people when, or among whom, the system could be tried with so good a hope of success. It was so long before we had been allowed to stand on our bottom, that the Fixed Period became a matter of common conversation in Britannula. There were many who looked forward to it as the creator of a new idea of wealth and comfort; and it was in those days that the calculation was made as to the rivers and railways. I think that in England they thought that a few, and but a few, among us were dreamers of a dream. Had they believed that the Fixed Period would ever have become law, they would not have permitted us to be law-makers. I acknowledge that. But when we were once independent, then again to reduce us to submission by a 250-ton steam-swiveller was an act of gross tyranny.

What should be the Fixed Period? That was the first question which demanded an immediate answer. Years were named absurd in their intended leniency ;—eighty and even eighty-five! Let us say a hundred, said I, aloud, turning upon them all the battery of my ridicule. I suggested sixty; but the term was received with silence. I pointed out that the few old men now on the island might be exempted, and that even those above fifty-five might be allowed to drag out their existences if they were weak enough to select for themselves so degrading a position. This latter proposition was accepted at once, and the exempt showed no repugnance even when it was proved to them that they would be left alone in the community and entitled to no honour, and never allowed even to enter the pleasant gardens of the college. I think now that sixty was too early an age, and that sixty-five, to which I gracefully yielded, is the proper Fixed Period for the human race. Let any man look among his friends and see whether men of sixty-five are not in the way of those

who are still aspiring to rise in the world.
A judge shall be deaf on the bench when
younger men below him can hear with accuracy. His voice shall have descended to a poor
treble, or his eyesight shall be dim and failing.
At any rate, his limbs will have lost all that
robust agility which is needed for the adequate
performance of the work of the world. It is
self-evident that at sixty-five a man has done
all that he is fit to do. He should be troubled
no longer with labour, and therefore should
be troubled no longer with life. "It is all
vanity and vexation of spirit," such a one
would say, if still brave, and still desirous
of honour. "Lead me into the college, and
there let me prepare myself for that brighter
life which will require no mortal strength."
My words did avail with many, and then
they demanded that seventy should be the
Fixed Period.

How long we fought over this point need
not now be told. But we decided at last to

divide the interval. Sixty-seven and a half was named by a majority of the Assembly as the Fixed Period. Surely the colony was determined to grow in truth old before it could go into the college. But then there came a further dispute. On which side of the Fixed Period should the year of grace be taken? Our debates even on this subject were long and animated. It was said that the seclusion within the college would be tantamount to penal departure, and that the old men should thus have the last lingering drops of breath allowed them, without, in the world at large. It was at last decided that men and· women should be brought into the college at sixty-seven, and that before their sixty-eighth birthday they should have departed. Then the bells were rung, and the whole community rejoiced, and banquets were eaten, and the young men and women called each other brother and sister, and it was felt that a great reform had been inaugurated among us for the benefit of mankind at large.

Little was thought about it at home in England when the bill was passed. There was, I suppose, in the estimation of Englishmen, time enough to think about it. The idea was so strange to them that it was considered impossible that we should carry it out. They heard of the bill, no doubt; but I maintain that, as we had been allowed to separate ourselves and stand alone, it was no more their concern than if it had been done in Arizona or Idaho, or any of those Western States of America which have lately formed themselves into a new union. It was from them, no doubt, that we chiefly expected that sympathy which, however, we did not receive. The world was clearly not yet alive to the grand things in store for it. We received, indeed, a violent remonstrance from the old-fashioned Government at Washington; but in answer to that we stated that we were prepared to stand

and fall by the new system—that we expected glory rather than ignominy, and to be followed by mankind rather than repudiated. We had a lengthened correspondence also with New Zealand and with Australia; but England at first did not believe us; and when she was given to understand that we were in earnest, she brought to bear upon us the one argument that could have force, and sent to our harbour her 250-ton steam-swiveller. The 250-ton swiveller, no doubt, was unanswerable — unless we were prepared to die for our system. I was prepared, but I could not carry the people of my country with me.

I have now given the necessary prelude to the story which I have to tell. I cannot but think that, in spite of the isolated manners of Great Britain, readers in that country generally must have become acquainted with the views of the Fixed-Periodists. It cannot but be that a scheme with such power to change, —and, I may say, to improve,—the manners and habits of mankind, should be known in a country in which a portion of the inhabitants do, at any rate, read and write. They boast, indeed, that not **a** man or a woman in the British Islands is now ignorant of his letters; but I am informed that the knowledge seldom approaches to any literary taste. It may be that a portion of the masses should have been ignorant of what was being done within the empire of the South Pacific. I have therefore written this preliminary chapter to explain to them what was the condition of Britannula in regard to the Fixed Period just twelve months before England had taken possession of us, and once more made us her own. Sir Ferdinando Brown now rules us, I must say, not with a rod of iron, but very much after his own good will. He makes us flowery speeches, and thinks that they will stand in lieu of independence. He collects his revenue, and informs us that to be taxed is the highest privilege of an ornate civilisation. He pointed to the gunboat in the bay when it came, and called it the divine depository of beneficent power. For a time, no doubt, British "tenderness" will prevail. But I shall have wasted my thoughts, and in vain poured out my eloquence as to the Fixed Period, if, in the course of years, it does not again spring to the front, and prove itself to be necessary before man can accomplish all that he is destined to achieve.

CHAPTER II.

GABRIEL CRASWELLER.

I WILL now begin my tale. It is above thirty years since I commenced my agitation in Britannula. We were a small people, and had not then been blessed by separation; but we were, I think, peculiarly intelligent. We were the very cream, as it were, that had been skimmed from the milk-pail of the people of a wider colony, themselves gifted with more than ordinary intelligence. We were the *élite* of the selected population of New Zealand. I think I may say that no race so well informed ever before set itself down to form a new nation. I am now nearly sixty years old,—very nearly fit for the college which, alas! will never be

open for me,—and I was nearly thirty when I
began to be in earnest as to the Fixed Period.
At that time my dearest friend and most
trusted coadjutor was Gabriel Crasweller. He
was ten years my senior then, and is now
therefore fit for deposition in the college were
the college there to receive him. He was one
of those who brought with them merino sheep
into the colony. At great labour and expense
he exported from New Zealand a small flock
of choice animals, with which he was successful from the first. He took possession of the
lands of Little Christchurch, five or six miles
from Gladstonopolis, and showed great judgment in the selection. A prettier spot, as it
turned out, for the fattening of both beef and
mutton and for the growth of wool, it would
have been impossible to have found. Everything that human nature wants was there
at Little Christchurch. The streams which
watered the land were bright and rapid, and
always running. The grasses were peculiarly

rich, and the old English fruit-trees, which we had brought with us from New Zealand, throve there with an exuberant fertility, of which the mother country, I am told, knows nothing. He had imported pheasants' eggs, and salmon-spawn, and young deer, and black-cock and grouse, and those beautiful little Alderney cows no bigger than good-sized dogs, which, when milked, give nothing but cream. All these things throve with him uncommonly, so that it may be declared of him that his lines had fallen in pleasant places. But he had no son; and therefore in discussing with him, as I did daily, the question of the Fixed Period, I promised him that it should be my lot to deposit him in the sacred college when the day of his withdrawal should have come. He had been married before we left New Zealand, and was childless when he made for himself and his wife his homestead at Little Christchurch. But there, after a few years, a daughter was born to him, and I ought to have remembered, when I promised to him that last act of friendship, that it might become the duty of that child's husband to do for him with filial reverence the loving work which I had undertaken to perform.

Many and most interesting were the conversations held between Crasweller and myself on the great subject which filled our hearts. He undoubtedly was sympathetic, and took delight in expatiating on all those benefits that would come to the world from the race of mankind which knew nothing of the debility of old age. He saw the beauty of the theory as well as did I myself, and would speak often of the weakness of that pretended tenderness which would fear to commence a new operation in regard to the feelings of the men and women of the old world. "Can any man love another better than I do you?" I would say to him with energy; "and yet would I scruple for a moment to deposit you in the college when the day had come? I should lead you in with that perfect reverence which it is impossible that the young should feel for the old when they become feeble and incapable." I doubt now whether he relished these allusions to his own seclusion. He would run away from his own individual case, and generalise widely about some future time. And when the time for voting came, he certainly did vote for seventy-five. But I took no offence at his vote. Gabriel Crasweller was almost my dearest friend, and as his girl grew up it was a matter of regret to me that my only son was not quite old enough to be her husband.

Eva Crasweller was, I think, the most perfect piece I ever beheld of youthful feminine beauty. I have not yet seen those English beauties of which so much is said in their own romances, but whom the young men from New York and San Francisco who make their way to Gladstonopolis do not seem to admire very much. Eva was perfect in symmetry, in features, in complexion, and in simplicity

of manners. All languages are the same to
her; but that accomplishment has become
so common in Britannula that but little is
thought of it. I do not know whether she
ravished our ears most with the old-fashioned
piano and the nearly obsolete violin, or with
the modern mousometor, or the more perfect
melpomeneon. It was wonderful to hear the
way with which she expressed herself at the
meeting held about the rising buildings of the
college when she was only sixteen. But I
think she touched me most with just a roly-
poly pudding which she made with her own
fair hands for our dinner one Sunday at Little
Christchurch. And once when I saw her by
chance take a kiss from her lover behind the
door, I felt that it was a pity indeed that a
man should ever become old. Perhaps, however,
in the eyes of some her brightest charm lay
in the wealth which her father possessed. His
sheep had greatly increased in number; the
valleys were filled with his cattle; and he

could always sell his salmon for half-a-crown a pound and his pheasants for seven-and-six-pence a brace. Everything had thriven with Crasweller, and everything must belong to Eva as soon as he should have been led into the college. Eva's mother was now dead, and no other child had been born. Crasweller had also embarked his money largely in the wool trade, and had become a sleeping-partner in the house of Grundle & Grabbe. He was an older man by ten years than either of his partners, but yet Grundle's eldest son Abraham was older than Eva when Crasweller lent his money to the firm. It was soon known who was to be the happiest man in the empire. It was young Abraham, by whom Eva was kissed behind the door that Sunday when we ate the roly-poly pudding. Then she came into the room, and, with her eyes raised to heaven, and with a halo of glory almost round her head as she poured forth her voice, she touched the mousometor, and gave us the Old Hundredth psalm.

She was a fine girl at all points, and had been quite alive to the dawn of the Fixed Period system. But at this time, on the memorable occasion of the eating of that dinner, it first began to strike me that my friend Crasweller was getting very near his Fixed Period, and it occurred to me to ask myself questions as to what might be the daughter's wishes. It was the state of her feelings rather that would push itself into my mind. Quite lately he had said nothing about it,—nor had she. On that Sunday morning when he and his girl were at church,—for Crasweller had stuck to the old habit of saying his prayers in a special place on a special day,—I had discussed the matter with young Grundle. Nobody had been into the college as yet. Three or four had died naturally, but Crasweller was about to be the first. We were arranging that he should be attended by pleasant visitors till within the last week or two, and I was making special allusion to the law which required that he should abandon all control of his property immediately on his entering the college. "I suppose he would do that," said Grundle, expressing considerable interest by the tone of his voice.

"Oh, certainly," said I; "he must do that in accordance with the law. But he can make his will up to the very moment in which he is deposited." He had then about twelve months to run. I suppose there was not a man or woman in the community who was not accurately aware of the very day of Crasweller's birth. We had already introduced the habit of tattooing on the backs of the babies the day on which they were born; and we had succeeded in operating also on many of the children who had come into the world before the great law. Some there were who would not submit on behalf of themselves or their children; and we did look forward to some little confusion in this matter. A register had of course been commenced, and there

were already those who refused to state their
exact ages ; but I had been long on the look-
out for this, and had a little book of my own in
which were inscribed the " periods " of all those
who had come to Britannula with us ; and
since I had first thought of the Fixed Period
I had been very careful to note faithfully
the births as they occurred. The reader will
see how important, as time went on, it would
become to have an accurate record, and I
already then feared that there might be some
want of fidelity after I myself had been deposited. But my friend Crasweller was the
first on the list, and there was no doubt in
the empire as to the exact day on which he
was born. All Britannula knew that he
would be the first, and that he was to be
deposited on the 13th of June 1980. In conversation with my friend I had frequently
alluded to the very day,—to the happy day,
as I used to call it before I became acquainted
with his actual feelings,—and he never ven-

tured to deny that on that day he would become sixty-seven.

I have attempted to describe his daughter Eva, and I must say a word as to the personal qualities of her father. He too was a remarkably handsome man, and though his hair was beautifully white, had fewer of the symptoms of age than any old man I had before known. He was tall, robust, and broad, and there was no beginning even of a stoop about him. He spoke always clearly and audibly, and he was known for the firm voice with which he would perform occasionally at some of our decimal readings. We had fixed our price at a decimal in order that the sum so raised might be used for the ornamentation of the college. Our population at Gladstonopolis was so thriving that we found it as easy to collect ten pennies as one. At these readings Gabriel Crasweller was the favourite performer, and it had begun to be whispered by some caitiffs who would willingly disarrange the whole starry system for their own immediate gratification, that Crasweller should not be deposited because of the beauty of his voice. And then the difficulty was somewhat increased by the care and precision with which he attended to his own business. He was as careful as ever about his flocks, and at shearing-time would stand all day in the wool-shed to see to the packing of his wool and the marking of his bales.

"It would be a pity," said to me a Britannulist one day,—a man younger than myself,— "to lock up old Crasweller, and let the business go into the hands of young Grundle. Young Grundle will never know half as much about sheep, in spite of his conceit; and Crasweller is a deal fitter for his work than for living idle in the college till you shall put an end to him."

There was much in these words which made me very angry. According to this man's feelings, the whole system was to be made to suit itself to the peculiarities of one individual constitution. A man who so spoke could have known nothing of the general beauty of the Fixed Period. And he had alluded to the manner of depositing in most disrespectful terms. I had felt it to be essentially necessary so to maintain the dignity of the ceremony as to make it appear as unlike an execution as possible. And this depositing of Crasweller was to be the first, and should—according to my own intentions—be attended with a peculiar grace and reverence. "I don't know what you call locking up," said I, angrily. "Had Mr Crasweller been about to be dragged to a felon's prison, you could not have used more opprobrious language; and as to putting an end to him, you must, I think, be ignorant of the method proposed for adding honour and glory to the last moments in this world of those dear friends whose happy lot it will be to be withdrawn from the world's troubles amidst the love and veneration of their fellow-subjects." As to the actual mode of transition, there·had been many discussions held by the executive in President Square, and it had at last been decided that certain veins should be opened while the departing one should, under the influence of morphine, be gently entranced within a warm bath. I, as president of the empire, had agreed to use the lancet in the first two or three cases, thereby intending to increase the honours conferred. Under these circumstances I did feel the sting bitterly when he spoke of my putting "an end" to him. "But you have not," I said, "at all realised the feeling of the ceremony. A few ill-spoken words, such as these you have just uttered, will do us more harm in the minds of many than all your voting will have done good." In answer to this he merely repeated his observation that Crasweller was a very bad specimen to begin with. "He has got ten years of work in him," said my friend, "and yet you intend to make away with him without the slightest compunction."

Make away with him! What an expression

to use,—and this from the mouth of one who had been a determined Fixed - Periodist! It angered me to think that men should be so little reasonable as to draw deductions as to an entire system from a single instance. Crasweller might in truth be strong and hearty at the Fixed Period. But that period had been chosen with reference to the community at large; and what though he might have to depart a year or two before he was worn out, still he would do so with everything around him to make him happy, and would depart before he had ever known the agony of a headache. Looking at the entire question with the eyes of reason, I could not but tell myself that a better example of a triumphant beginning to our system could not have been found. But yet there was in it something unfortunate. Had our first hero been compelled to abandon his business by old age—had he become doting over its details—parsimonious, or extravagant, or even short - sighted in his speculations—

public feeling, than which nothing is more ignorant, would have risen in favour of the Fixed Period. "How true is the president's reasoning," the people would have said. "Look at Crasweller; he would have ruined Little Christchurch had he stayed there much longer." But everything he did seemed to prosper; and it occurred to me at last that he forced himself into abnormal sprightliness, with a view of bringing disgrace upon the law of the Fixed Period. If there were any such feeling, I regard it as certainly mean.

On the day after the dinner at which Eva's pudding was eaten, Abraham Grundle came to me at the Executive Hall, and said that he had a few things to discuss with me of importance. Abraham was a good-looking young man, with black hair and bright eyes, and a remarkably handsome moustache; and he was one well inclined to business, in whose hands the firm of Grundle, Grabbe, & Crasweller was likely to thrive; but I myself had never liked him much. I had thought him to be a little wanting in that reverence which he owed to his elders, and to be, moreover, somewhat over-fond of money. It had leaked out that though he was no doubt attached to Eva Crasweller, he had thought quite as much of Little Christ-church; and though he could kiss Eva behind the door, after the ways of young men, still he was more intent on the fleeces than on her lips. "I want to say a word to you, Mr President," he began, "upon a subject that disturbs my conscience very much"

"Your conscience?" said I.

"Yes, Mr President. I believe you're aware that I am engaged to marry Miss Crasweller?"

It may be as well to explain here that my own eldest son, as fine a boy as ever delighted a mother's eye, was only two years younger than Eva, and that my wife, Mrs Neverbend, had of late got it into her head that he was quite old enough to marry the girl. It was in vain that I told her that all that had been settled while

Jack was still at the didascalion. He had been Colonel of the Curriculum, as they now call the head boy; but Eva had not then cared for Colonels of Curriculums, but had thought more of young Grundle's moustache. My wife declared that all that was altered,—that Jack was, in fact, a much more manly fellow than Abraham with his shiny bit of beard; and that if one could get at a maiden's heart, we should find that Eva thought so. In answer to this I bade her hold her tongue, and remember that in Britannula a promise was always held to be as good as a bond. "I suppose a young woman may change her mind in Britannula as well as elsewhere," said my wife. I turned all this over in my mind, because the slopes of Little Christchurch are very alluring, and they would all belong to Eva so soon. And then it would be well, as I was about to perform for Crasweller so important a portion of his final ceremony, our close intimacy should be drawn still nearer by a family connection.

I did think of it ; but then it occurred
to me that the girl's engagement to young
Grundle was an established fact, and it did
not behove me to sanction the breach of a
contract. "Oh yes," said I to the young man,
"I am aware that there is an understanding
to that effect between you and Eva's father"

"And between me and Eva, I can assure
you"

Having observed the kiss behind the door on
the previous day, I could not deny the truth of
this assertion.

"It is quite understood," continued Abraham,
"and I had always thought that it was to take
place at once, so that Eva might get used to
her new life before her papa was deposited."

To this I merely bowed my head, as though
to signify that it was a matter with which I
was not personally concerned. "I had taken
it for granted that my old friend would like
to see his daughter settled, and Little Christchurch put into his daughter's hands before he

should bid adieu to his own sublunary affairs," I remarked, when I found that he paused.

"We all thought so up at the warehouse," said he,—"I and father, and Grabbe, and Postlecott, our chief clerk. Postlecott is the next but three on the books, and is getting very melancholy. But he is especially anxious just at present to see how Crasweller bears it."

"What has all that to do with Eva's marriage?"

"I suppose I might marry her. But he hasn't made any will."

"What does that matter? There is nobody to interfere with Eva."

"But he might go off, Mr Neverbend," whispered Grundle; "and where should I be then? If he was to get across to Auckland, or to Sydney, and to leave some one to manage the property for him, what could you do? That's what I want to know. The law says that he shall be deposited on a certain day"

"He will become as nobody in the eye of

the law," said I, with all the authority of a President.

"But if he and his daughter have understood each other; and if some deed be forthcoming by which Little Christchurch shall have been left to trustees; and if he goes on living at Sydney, let us say, on the fat of the land,— drawing all the income, and leaving the trustees as legal owners,—where should I be then?"

"In that case," said I, having taken two or three minutes for consideration,—"in that case, I presume the property would be confiscated by law, and would go to his natural heir. Now if his natural heir be then your wife, it will be just the same as though the property were yours." Young Grundle shook his head. "I don't know what more you would want. At any rate, there is no more for you to get." I confess that at that moment the idea of my boy's chance of succeeding with the heiress did present itself to my mind. According to what my wife had said, Jack would have jumped at the girl with just what she stood up in; and had sworn to his mother, when he had been told that morning about the kiss behind the door, that he would knock that brute's head off his shoulders before many days were gone by. Looking at the matter merely on behalf of Jack, it appeared to me that Little Christchurch would, in that case, be quite safe, let Crasweller be deposited,—or run away to Sydney.

"You do not know for certain about the confiscation of the property," said Abraham.

"I've told you as much, Mr Grundle, as it is fit that you should know," I replied, with severity. "For the absolute condition of the law you must look in the statute-book, and not come to the President of the empire."

Abraham Grundle then departed. I had assumed an angry air, as though I were offended with him, for troubling me on a matter by referring simply to an individual. But he had in truth given rise to very serious and solemn thoughts. Could it be that Crasweller, my own confidential friend—the man to whom I had trusted the very secrets of my soul on this important matter,—could it be that he should be unwilling to be deposited when the day had come? Could it be that he should be anxious to fly from his country and her laws, just as the time had arrived when those laws might operate upon him for the benefit of that country? I could not think that he was so vain, so greedy, so selfish, and so unpatriotic. But this was not all. Should he attempt to fly, could we prevent his flying? And if he did fly, what step should we take next? The Government of New South Wales was hostile to us on the very matter of the Fixed Period, and certainly would not surrender him in obedience to any law of extradition. And he might leave his property to trustees who would manage it on his behalf; although, as far as Britannula was concerned, he would be beyond the reach of law, and regarded even as being without the pale of life. And if he, the first of the Fixed-

Periodists, were to run away, the fashion of so running would become common. We should thus be rid of our old men, and our object would be so far attained. But looking forward, I could see at a glance that if one or two wealthy members of our community were thus to escape, it would be almost impossible to carry out the law with reference to those who should have no such means. But that which vexed me most was that Gabriel Crasweller should desire to escape,—that he should be anxious to throw over the whole system to preserve the poor remnant of his life. If he would do so, who could be expected to abstain? If he should prove false when the moment came, who would prove true? And he, the first, the very first on our list! Young Grundle had now left me, and as I sat thinking of it I was for a moment tempted to abandon the Fixed Period altogether. But as I remained there in silent meditation, better thoughts came to me. Had I dared to regard myself as

the foremost spirit of my age, and should 1
thus be turned back by the human weakness
of one poor creature who had not sufficiently
collected the strength of his heart to be able to
look death in the face and to laugh him down.
It was a difficulty—a difficulty the more. It
might be the crushing difficulty which would
put an end to the system as far as my existence was concerned. But I bethought me how
many early reformers had perished in their
efforts, and how seldom it had been given to
the first man to scale the walls of prejudice,
and force himself into the citadel of reason.
But they had not yielded when things had
gone against them; and though they had not
brought their visions down to the palpable touch
of humanity, still they had persevered, and their
efforts had not been altogether lost to the world.

"So it shall be with me," said I. "Though
I may never live to deposit a human being
within that sanctuary, and though I may be
doomed by the foolish prejudice of men to

drag out a miserable existence amidst the sor-
rows and weakness of old age ; though it may
never be given to me to feel the ineffable
comforts of a triumphant deposition,—still my
name will be handed down to coming ages,
and I shall be spoken of as the first who
endeavoured to save grey hairs from being
brought with sorrow to the grave."

I am now writing on board H.M. gunboat
John Bright,—for the tyrannical slaves of a
modern monarch have taken me in the flesh
and are carrying me off to England, so that,
as they say, all that nonsense of a Fixed
Period may die away in Britannula.   They
think,—poor ignorant fighting men,—that such
a theory can be made to perish because one
individual shall have been mastered.   But no !
The idea will still live, and in ages to come
men will prosper and be strong, and thrive,
unpolluted by the greed and cowardice of
second childhood, because John Neverbend
was at one time President of Britannula.

It occurred to me then, as I sat meditating over the tidings conveyed to me by Abraham Grundle, that it would be well that I should see Crasweller, and talk to him freely on the subject. It had sometimes been that by my strength I had reinvigorated his halting courage. This suggestion that he might run away as the day of his deposition drew nigh,—or rather, that others might run away,—had been the subject of some conversation between him and me. "How will it be," he had said, "if they mizzle?" He had intended to allude to the possible premature departure of those who were about to be deposited.

"Men will never be so weak," I said.

"I suppose you'd take all their property?"

"Every stick of it."

"But property is a thing which can be conveyed away."

"We should keep a sharp look-out upon themselves. There might be a writ, you know, *ne exeant regno.* If we are driven to a pinch, that will be the last thing to do. But I should be sorry to be driven to express my fear of human weakness by any general measure of that kind. It would be tantamount to an accusation of cowardice against the whole empire."

Crasweller had only shaken his head. But I had understood him to shake it on the part of the human race generally, and not on his own behalf.

CHAPTER III.

THE FIRST BREAK-DOWN.

IT was now mid-winter, and it wanted just twelve months to that 30th of June on which, in accordance with all our plans, Crasweller was to be deposited. A full year would, no doubt, suffice for him to arrange his worldly affairs, and to see his daughter married; but it would not more than suffice. He still went about his business with an alacrity marvellous in one who was so soon about to withdraw himself from the world. The fleeces for bearing which he was preparing his flocks, though they might be shorn by him, would never return their prices to his account. They would do so for his daughter and his son-in-law; but in these circumstances, it would have been well for him to have left the flocks to his son-in-law, and to have turned his mind to the consideration of other matters. "There should be a year devoted to that final year to be passed within the college, so that, by degrees, the mind may be weaned from the ignoble art of money-making." I had once so spoken to him; but there he was, as intent as ever, with his mind fixed on the records of the price of wool as they came back to him from the English and American markets. "It is all for his daughter," I had said to myself. "Had he been blessed with a son, it would have been otherwise with him" So I got on to my steam-tricycle, and in a few minutes I was at Little Christchurch. He was coming in after a hard day's work among the flocks, and seemed to be triumphant and careful at the same time.

"I tell you what it is, Neverbend," said he; "we shall have the fluke over here if we don't look after ourselves"

"Have you found symptoms of it?"

"Well; not exactly among my own sheep; but I know the signs of it so well. My grasses are peculiarly dry, and my flocks are remarkably well looked after; but I can see indications of it. Only fancy where we should all be if fluke showed itself in Britannula! If it once got ahead we should be no better off than the Australians."

This might be anxiety for his daughter; but it looked strangely like that personal feeling which would have been expected in him twenty years ago. "Crasweller," said I, "do you mind coming into the house, and having a little chat?" and so I got off my tricycle.

"I was going to be very busy," he said, showing an unwillingness. "I have fifty young foals in that meadow there; and I like to see that they get their suppers served to them warm."

"Bother the young foals!" said I. "As if

you had not men enough about the place to
see to feeding your stock without troubling
yourself. I have come out from Gladstonopolis, because I want to see you; and now
I am to be sent back in order that you might
attend to the administration of hot mashes!
Come into the house." Then I entered in
under the verandah, and he followed. "You
certainly have got the best-furnished house
in the empire," said I, as I threw myself on
to a double arm-chair, and lighted my cigar
in the inner verandah.

"Yes, yes," said he; "it is pretty comfortable."

He was evidently melancholy, and knew
the purpose for which I had come. "I don't
suppose any girl in the old country was ever
better provided for than will be Eva." This
I said wishing to comfort him, and at the
same time to prepare for what was to be said.

"Eva is a good girl,—a dear girl. But I
am not at all so sure about that young fellow

Abraham Grundle. It's a pity, President, your son had not been born a few years sooner." At this moment my boy was half a head taller than young Grundle, and a much better specimen of a Britannulist. "But it is too late now, I suppose, to talk of that. It seems to me that Jack never even thinks of looking at Eva."

This was a view of the case which certainly was strange to me, and seemed to indicate that Crasweller was gradually becoming fit for the college. If he could not see that Jack was madly in love with Eva, he could see nothing at all. But I had not come out to Little Christchurch at the present moment to talk to him about the love matters of the two children. I was intent on something of infinitely greater importance. "Crasweller," said I, "you and I have always agreed to the letter on this great matter of the Fixed Period." He looked into my face with supplicating, weak eyes, but he said nothing. "Your period now will soon have been reached, and I think it well that we, as dear loving friends, should learn to discuss the matter closely as it draws nearer. I do not think that it becomes either of us to be afraid of it."

"That's all very well for you," he replied. "I am your senior."

"Ten years, I believe."

"About nine, I think."

This might have come from a mistake of his as to my exact age; and though I was surprised at the error, I did not notice it on this occasion. "You have no objection to the law as it stands now?" I said.

"It might have been seventy."

"That has all been discussed fully, and you have given your assent. Look round on the men whom you can remember, and tell me, on how many of them life has not sat as a burden at seventy years of age?"

"Men are so different," said he "As far as one can judge of his own capacities, I was never better able to manage my business than

I am at present. It is more than I can say for that young fellow Grundle, who is so anxious to step into my shoes."

"My dear Crasweller," I rejoined, "it was out of the question so to arrange the law as to vary the term to suit the peculiarities of one man or another."

"But in a change of such terrible severity you should have suited the eldest."

This was dreadful to me,—that he, the first to receive at the hands of his country the great honour intended for him,—that he should have already allowed his mind to have rebelled against it! If he, who had once been so keen a supporter of the Fixed Period, now turned round and opposed it, how could others who should follow be expected to yield themselves up in a fitting frame of mind? And then I spoke my thoughts freely to him. "Are you afraid of departure?" I said,—"afraid of that which must come; afraid to meet as a friend that which you must meet so soon as friend or enemy?" I paused; but he sat looking at me without reply. " To fear departure;—must it not be the greatest evil of all our life, if it be necessary? Can God have brought us into the world, intending us so to leave it that the very act of doing so shall be regarded by us as a curse so terrible as to neutralise all the blessings of our existence? Can it be that He who created us should have intended that we should so regard our dismissal from the world? The teachers of religion have endeavoured to reconcile us to it, and have, in their vain zeal, endeavoured to effect it by picturing to our imaginations a hell-fire into which ninety-nine must fall; while one shall be allowed to escape to a heaven, which is hardly made more alluring to us! Is that the way to make a man comfortable at the prospect of leaving this world? But it is necessary to our dignity as men that we shall find the mode of doing so. To lie quivering and quaking on my bed at the expectation of the Black Angel of Death, does not suit my manhood,—which would fear nothing;—which does not, and shall not, stand in awe of aught but my own sins. How best shall we prepare ourselves for the day which we know cannot be avoided? That is the question which I have ever been asking myself,—which you and I have asked ourselves, and which I thought we had answered. Let us turn the inevitable into that which shall in itself be esteemed a glory to us. Let us teach the world so to look forward with longing eyes, and not with a faint heart. I had thought to have touched some few, not by the eloquence of my words, but by the energy of my thoughts; and you, oh my friend, have ever been he whom it has been my greatest joy to have had with me as the sharer of my aspirations."

"But I am nine years older than you are."

I again passed by the one year added to my age. There was nothing now in so trifling an error. "But you still agree with me as to the fundamental truth of our doctrine."

"I suppose so," said Crasweller.

"I suppose so!" repeated I. "Is that all that can be said for the philosophy to which we have devoted ourselves, and in which nothing false can be found?"

"It won't teach any one to think it better to live than to die while he is fit to perform all the functions of life. It might be very well if you could arrange that a man should be deposited as soon as he becomes absolutely infirm."

"Some men are infirm at forty."

"Then deposit them," said Crasweller.

"Yes; but they will not own that they are infirm. If a man be weak at that age, he thinks that with advancing years he will resume the strength of his youth. There must, in fact, be a Fixed Period. We have discussed that fifty times, and have always arrived at the same conclusion."

He sat still, silent, unhappy, and confused. I saw that there was something on his mind to which he hardly dared to give words. Wishing to encourage him, I went on. "After all, you have a full twelve months yet before the day shall have come."

"Two years," he said, doggedly.

"Exactly; two years before your departure, but twelve months before deposition."

"Two years before deposition," said Crasweller.

At this I own I was astonished. Nothing was better known in the empire than the ages of the two or three first inhabitants to be deposited. I would have undertaken to declare that not a man or a woman in Britannula was in doubt as to Mr Crasweller's exact age. It had been written in the records, and upon the stones belonging to the college. There was no doubt that within twelve months of the present date he was due to be detained there as the first inhabitant. And now I was astounded to hear him claim another year, which could not be allowed him.

"That impudent fellow Grundle has been

with me," he continued, "and wishes to make me believe that he can get rid of me in one year. I have, at any rate, two years left of my out-of-door existence, and I do not mean to give up a day of it for Grundle or any one else."

It was something to see that he still recognised the law, though he was so meanly anxious to evade it. There had been some whisperings in the empire among the elderly men and women of a desire to obtain the assistance of Great Britain in setting it aside. Peter Grundle, for instance, Crasweller's senior partner, had been heard to say that England would not allow a deposited man to be slaughtered. There was much in that which had angered me. The word slaughter was in itself peculiarly objectionable to my ears,—to me who had undertaken to perform the first ceremony as an act of grace. And what had England to do with our laws? It was as though Russia were to turn upon the United

States and declare that their Congress should be put down. What would avail the loudest voice of Great Britain against the smallest spark of a law passed by our Assembly?— unless, indeed, Great Britain should condescend to avail herself of her great power, and thus to crush the free voice of those whom she had already recognised as independent. As I now write, this is what she has already done, and history will have to tell the story. But it was especially sad to have to think that there should be a Britannulist so base, such a coward, such a traitor, as himself to propose this expedient for adding a few years to his own wretched life.

But Crasweller did not, as it seemed, intend to avail himself of these whispers. His mind was intent on devising some falsehood by which he should obtain for himself just one other year of life, and his expectant son-in-law purposed to prevent him. I hardly knew as I turned it all in my mind, which of the two was the more sordid; but I think that my sympathies were rather in accord with the cowardice of the old man than with the greed of the young. After all, I had known from the beginning that the fear of death was a human weakness. To obliterate that fear from the human heart, and to build up a perfect manhood that should be liberated from so vile a thraldom, had been one of the chief objects of my scheme. I had no right to be angry with Crasweller, because Crasweller, when tried, proved himself to be no stronger than the world at large. It was a matter to me of infinite regret that it should be so. He was the very man, the very friend, on whom I had relied with confidence! But his weakness was only a proof that I myself had been mistaken. In all that Assembly by which the law had been passed, consisting chiefly of young men, was there one on whom I could rest with confidence to carry out the purpose of the law when his own time should come?

Ought I not so to have arranged matters that I myself should have been the first,—to have postponed the use of the college till such time as I might myself have been deposited? This had occurred to me often throughout the whole agitation; but then it had occurred also that none might perhaps follow me, when under such circumstances I should have departed!

But in my heart I could forgive Crasweller. For Grundle I felt nothing but personal dislike. He was anxious to hurry on the deposition of his father-in-law, in order that the entire possession of Little Christchurch might come into his own hands just one year the earlier! No doubt he knew the exact age of the man as well as I did, but it was not for him to have hastened his deposition. And then I could not but think, even in this moment of public misery, how willing Jack would have been to have assisted old Crasweller in his little fraud, so that Eva might have been the reward. My belief is that he would have sworn against his

own father, perjured himself in the very teeth
of truth, to have obtained from Eva that little
privilege which I had once seen Grundle enjoying.

I was sitting there silent in Crasweller's
verandah as all this passed through my mind.
But before I spoke again I was enabled to see
clearly what duty required of me. Eva and
Little Christchurch, with Jack's feelings and
interests, and all my wife's longings, must be
laid on one side, and my whole energy must be
devoted to the literal carrying out of the law.
It was a great world's movement that had been
projected, and if it were to fail now, just at its
commencement, when everything had been arranged for the work, when again would there
be hope? It was a matter which required
legislative sanction in whatever country might
adopt it. No despot could attempt it, let his
power be ever so confirmed. The whole country would rise against him when informed, in
its ignorance, of the contemplated intention.

Nor could it be effected by any congress of which the large majority were not at any rate under forty years of age. I had seen enough of human nature to understand its weakness in this respect. All circumstances had combined to make it practicable in Britannula, but all these circumstances might never be combined again. And it seemed to me to depend now entirely on the power which I might exert in creating courage in the heart of the poor timid creature who sat before me. I did know that were Britannula to appeal aloud to England, England, with that desire for interference which has always characterised her, would interfere. But if the empire allowed the working of the law to be commenced in silence, then the Fixed Period might perhaps be regarded as a thing settled. How much, then, depended on the words which I might use!

"Crasweller," I said, "my friend, my brother!"

"I don't know much about that. A man ought not to be so anxious to kill his brother."

"If I could take your place, as God will be my judge, I would do so with as ready a step as a young man to the arms of his beloved. And if for myself, why not for my brother?"

"You do not know," he said. "You have not, in truth, been tried."

"Would that you could try me!"

"And we are not all made of such stuff as you. You have talked about this till you have come to be in love with deposition and departure. But such is not the natural condition of a man. Look back upon all the centuries, and you will perceive that life has ever been dear to the best of men. And you will perceive also that they who have brought themselves to suicide have encountered the contempt of their fellow-creatures."

I would not tell him of Cato and Brutus, feeling that I could not stir him to grandeur of heart by Roman instances. He would have told me that in those days, as far as the Romans knew,

"the Everlasting had not fixed
His canon 'gainst self-slaughter."

I must reach him by other methods than these,
if at all. "Who can be more alive than you," I
said, "to the fact that man, by the fear of death,
is degraded below the level of the brutes?"

"If so, he is degraded," said Crasweller. "It
is his condition."

"But need he remain so? Is it not for you
and me to raise him to a higher level?"

"Not for me—not for me, certainly. I own
that I am no more than man. Little Christchurch is so pleasant to me, and Eva's smiles
and happiness; and the lowing of my flocks
and the bleating of my sheep are so gracious in
my ears, and it is so sweet to my eyes to see
how fairly I have turned this wilderness into a
paradise, that I own that I would fain stay
here a little longer."

"But the law, my friend, the law,—the law
which you yourself have been so active in
creating."

"The law allows me two years yet," said he; that look of stubbornness which I had before observed again spreading itself over his face.

Now this was a lie; an absolute, undoubted, demonstrable lie. And yet it was a lie which, by its mere telling, might be made available for its intended purpose. If it were known through the capital that Crasweller was anxious to obtain a year's grace by means of so foul a lie, the year's grace would be accorded to him. And then the Fixed Period would be at an end.

"I will tell you what it is," said he, anxious to represent his wishes to me in another light. "Grundle wants to get rid of me."

"Grundle, I fear, has truth on his side," said I, determined to show him that I, at any rate, would not consent to lend myself to the furtherance of a falsehood.

"Grundle wants to get rid of me," he repeated in the same tone. "But he shan't find that I am so easy to deal with. Eva already does not above half like him. Eva thinks that this depositing plan is abominable. She says that no good Christians ever thought of it."

"A child—a sweet child—but still only a child; and brought up by her mother with all the old prejudices."

"I don't know much about that. I never knew a decent woman who wasn't an Episcopalian. Eva is at any rate a good girl, to endeavour to save her father; and I'll tell you what—it is not too late yet. As far as my opinion goes, Jack Neverbend is ten to one a better sort of fellow than Abraham Grundle. Of course a promise has been made; but promises are like pie-crusts. Don't you think that Jack Neverbend is quite old enough to marry a wife, and that he only needs be told to make up his mind to do it? Little Christchurch would do just as well for him as for Grundle If he don't think much of the girl he must think something of the sheep."

Not think much of the girl! Just at this time Jack was talking to his mother, morning, noon, and night, about Eva, and threatening young Grundle with all kinds of schoolboy punishments if he should persevere in his suit. Only yesterday he had insulted Abraham grossly, and, as I had reason to suspect, had been more than once out to Christchurch on some clandestine object, as to which it was necessary, he thought, to keep old Crasweller in the dark. And then to be told in this manner that Jack didn't think much of Eva, and should be encouraged in preference to look after the sheep! He would have sacrificed every sheep on the place for the sake of half an hour with Eva alone in the woods. But he was afraid of Crasweller, whom he knew to have sanctioned an engagement with Abraham Grundle.

"I don't think that we need bring Jack and his love into this dispute," said I.

"Only that it isn't too late, you know.

Do you think that Jack could be brought to lend an ear to it?"

Perish Jack! perish Eva! perish Jack's mother, before I would allow myself to be bribed in this manner, to abandon the great object of all my life! This was evidently Crasweller's purpose. He was endeavouring to tempt me with his flocks and herds. The temptation, had he known it, would have been with Eva,—with Eva and the genuine, down-right, honest love of my gallant boy. I knew, too, that at home I should not dare to tell my wife that the offer had been made to me and had been refused. My wife could not understand,—Crasweller could not understand, —how strong may be the passion founded on the conviction of a life. And honesty, simple honesty, would forbid it. For me to strike a bargain with one already destined for deposi-tion,—that he should be withdrawn from his glorious, his almost immortal state, on the payment of a bribe to me and my family!

I had called this man my friend and brother, but how little had the man known me! Could I have saved all Gladstonopolis from imminent flames by yielding an inch in my convictions, I would not have done so in my then frame of mind; and yet this man,—my friend and brother,—had supposed that I could be bought to change my purpose by the pretty slopes and fat flocks of Little Christchurch!

"Crasweller," said I, "let us keep these two things separate; or rather, in discussing the momentous question of the Fixed Period, let us forget the loves of a boy and a girl."

"But the sheep, and the oxen, and the pastures! I can still make my will."

"The sheep, and the oxen, and the pastures must also be forgotten. They can have nothing to do with the settlement of this matter. My boy is dear to me, and Eva is dear also, but not to save even their young lives could I consent to a falsehood in this matter."

"Falsehood! There is no falsehood intended."

" Then there need be no bargain as to Eva, and no need for discussing the flocks and herds on this occasion. Crasweller, you are sixty-six now, and will be sixty-seven this time next year. Then the period of your deposition will have arrived, and in the year following,—two years hence, mind,—the Fixed Period of your departure will have come."

" No."

" Is not such the truth ? "

" No ; you put it all on a year too far. I was never more than nine years older than you. I remember it all as well as though it were yesterday when we first agreed to come away from New Zealand. When will you have to be deposited ? "

" In 1989," I said carefully. " My Fixed Period is 1990."

" Exactly ; and mine is nine years earlier. It always was nine years earlier."

It was all manifestly untrue. He knew it to be untrue. For the sake of one poor year

he was imploring my assent to a base falsehood, and was endeavouring to add strength to
his prayer by a bribe. How could I talk to
a man who would so far descend from the dignity of manhood? The law was there to support me, and the definition of the law was in
this instance supported by ample evidence.
I need only go before the executive of which
I myself was the chief, desire that the established documents should be searched, and de-
mand the body of Gabriel Crasweller to be
deposited in accordance with the law as enacted. But there was no one else to whom I
could leave the performance of this invidious
task, as a matter of course. There were alder-
men in Gladstonopolis and magistrates in the
country whose duty it would no doubt be to
see that the law was carried out. Arrangements to this effect had been studiously made
by myself. Such arrangements would no
doubt be carried out when the working of
the Fixed Period had become a thing estab-

lished. But I had long foreseen that the first deposition should be effected with some *éclat* of voluntary glory. It would be very detrimental to the cause to see my special friend Craswetter hauled away to the college by constables through the streets of Gladstonopolis, protesting that he was forced to his doom twelve months before the appointed time. Craswetter was a popular man in Britannula, and the people around would not be so conversant with the fact as was I, nor would they have the same reasons to be anxious that the law should be accurately followed. And yet how much depended upon the accuracy of following the law! A willing obedience was especially desired in the first instance, and a willing obedience I had expected from my friend Craswetter.

"Craswetter," I said, addressing him with great solemnity; "it is not so."

"It is—it is; I say it is."

"It is not so. The books that have been

printed and sworn to, which have had your own assent with that of others, are all against you."

"It was a mistake. I have got a letter from my old aunt in Hampshire, written to my mother when I was born, which proves the mistake."

"I remember the letter well," I said,—for we had all gone through such documents in performing the important task of settling the Period. "You were born in New South Wales, and the old lady in England did not write till the following year."

"Who says so? How can you prove it? She wasn't at all the woman to let a year go by before she congratulated her sister."

"We have your own signature affirming the date."

"How was I to know when I was born? All that goes for nothing."

"And unfortunately," said I, as though clenching the matter, "the Bible exists in which your father entered the date with his usual exemplary accuracy." Then he was silent for a moment as though having no further evidence to offer. "Crasweller," said I, "are you not man enough to do this thing in a straightforward, manly manner?"

"One year!" he exclaimed. "I only ask for one year. I do think that, as the first victim, I have a right to expect that one year should be granted me. Then Jack Neverbend shall have Little Christchurch, and the sheep, and the cattle, and Eva also, as his own for ever and ever,—or at any rate till he too shall be led away to execution!"

A victim; and execution! What language in which to speak of the great system! For myself I was determined that though I would be gentle with him I would not yield an inch. The law at any rate was with me, and I did not think as yet that Crasweller would lend himself to those who spoke of inviting the interference of England. The law was on my side, and so must still be all those who in the Assembly had voted for the Fixed Period. There had been enthusiasm then, and the different clauses had been carried by large majorities. A dozen different clauses had been carried, each referring to various branches of the question. Not only had the period been fixed, but money had been voted for the college; and the mode of life at the college had been settled; the very amusements of the old men had been sanctioned; and last, but not least, the very manner of departure had been fixed. There was the college now, a graceful building surrounded by growing shrubs and broad pleasant walks for the old men, endowed with a kitchen in which their taste should be consulted, and with a chapel for such of those who would require to pray in public; and all this would be made a laughing-stock to Britannula, if this old man Crasweller declined to enter the gates. "It must be done," I said in a tone of firm decision.

" No ! " he exclaimed.

" Crasweller, it must be done. The law demands it."

" No, no; not by me. You and young Grundle together are in a conspiracy to get rid of me. I am not going to be shut up a whole year before my time."

With that he stalked into the inner house, leaving me alone on the verandah. I had nothing for it but to turn on the electric lamp of my tricycle and steam back to Government House at Gladstonopolis with a sad heart.

CHAPTER IV.

JACK NEVERBEND.

SIX months passed away, which, I must own,
to me was a period of great doubt and un-
happiness, though it was relieved by certain
moments of triumph. Of course, as the time
drew nearer, the question of Crasweller's deposition became generally discussed by the
public of Gladstonopolis. And so also did
the loves of Abraham Grundle and Eva Crasweller. There were "Evaites" and "Abraham-
ites" in the community; for though the match
had not yet been altogether broken, it was known
that the two young people differed altogether
on the question of the old man's deposition.
It was said by the defendents of Grundle, who

were to be found for the most part among the young men and young women, that Abraham was simply anxious to carry out the laws of his country. It happened that, during this period, he was elected to a vacant seat in the Assembly, so that, when the matter came on for discussion there, he was able to explain publicly his motives; and it must be owned that he did so with good words and with a certain amount of youthful eloquence. As for Eva, she was simply intent on preserving the lees of her father's life, and had been heard to express an opinion that the college was "all humbug," and that people ought to be allowed to live as long as it pleased God to let them. Of course she had with her the elderly ladies of the community, and among them my own wife as the foremost. Mrs Neverbend had never made herself prominent before in any public question; but on this she seemed to entertain a very warm opinion. Whether this arose entirely from her desire to promote Jack's welfare, or from a reflection that her own period of deposition was gradually becoming nearer, I never could quite make up my mind. She had, at any rate, ten years to run, and I never heard from her any expressed fear of, — departure. She was,—and is,—a brave, good woman, attached to her household duties, anxious for her husband's comfort, but beyond measure solicitous for all good things to befall that scapegrace Jack Neverbend, for whom she thinks that nothing is sufficiently rich or sufficiently grand. Jack is a handsome boy, I grant, but that is about all that can be said of him; and in this matter he has been diametrically opposed to his father from first to last.

It will be seen that, in such circumstances, none of these moments of triumph to which I have alluded can have come to me within my own home. There Mrs Neverbend and Jack, and after a while Eva, sat together in perpetual council against me. When these meetings first began, Eva still acknowledged herself to be the promised bride of Abraham Grundle. There were her own vows, and her parent's assent, and something perhaps of remaining love. But presently she whispered to my wife that she could not but feel horror for the man who was anxious to "murder her father;" and by-and-by she began to own that she thought Jack a fine fellow. We had a wonderful cricket club in Gladstonopolis, and Britannula had challenged the English cricketers to come and play on the Little Christchurch ground, which they declared to be the only cricket ground as yet prepared on the face of the earth which had all the accomplishments possible for the due prosecution of the game. Now Jack, though very young, was captain of the club, and devoted much more of his time to that occupation than to his more legitimate business as a merchant. Eva, who had not hitherto paid much attention to cricket, became on a sudden passionately devoted to it; whereas Abraham Grundle, with a steadiness beyond his years, gave himself up more than ever to the business of the Assembly, and expressed some contempt for the game, though he was no mean player.

It had become necessary during this period to bring forward in the Assembly the whole question of the Fixed Period, as it was felt that, in the present state of public opinion, it would not be expedient to carry out the established law without the increased sanction which would be given to it by a further vote in the House. Public opinion would have forbidden us to deposit Crasweller without some such further authority. Therefore it was deemed necessary that a question should be asked, in which Crasweller's name was not mentioned, but which might lead to some general debate. Young Grundle demanded one morning whether it was the intention of the Government to see that the different clauses as to the new law respecting depositions were at once carried out. "The House is aware, I believe," he said, "that the first operation will soon be needed."

I may as well state here that this was repeated
to Eva, and that she pretended to take huff at
such a question from her lover. It was most
indecent, she said ; and she, after such words,
must drop him for ever. It was not for some
months after that, that she allowed Jack's
name to be mentioned with her own; but I
was aware that it was partly settled between
her and Jack and Mrs Neverbend. Grundle
declared his intention of proceeding against
old Crasweller in reference to the breach of
contract, according to the laws of Britannula ;
but that Jack's party disregarded altogether.
In telling this, however, I am advancing a
little beyond the point in my story to which I
have as yet carried my reader.

Then there arose a debate upon the whole
principle of the measure, which was carried
on with great warmth. I, as President, of
course took no part in it; but, in accordance
with our constitution, I heard it all from
the chair which I usually occupied at the

Speaker's right hand. The arguments on which the greatest stress was laid tended to show that the Fixed Period had been carried chiefly with a view to relieving the miseries of the old. And it was conclusively shown that, in a very great majority of cases, life beyond sixty-eight was all vanity and vexation of spirit. That other argument as to the costliness of old men to the state was for the present dropped. Had you listened to young Grundle, insisting with all the vehemence of youth on the absolute wretchedness to which the aged had been condemned by the absence of any such law,—had you heard the miseries of rheumatism, gout, stone, and general debility pictured in the eloquent words of five-and-twenty,—you would have felt that all who could lend themselves to perpetuate such a state of things must be guilty of fiendish cruelty. He really rose to a great height of parliamentary excellence, and altogether carried with him the younger, and luckily the greater, part of the House. There was really nothing to be said on the other side, except a repetition of the prejudices of the Old World But, alas! so strong are the weaknesses of the world, that prejudice can always vanquish truth by the mere strength of its battalions. Not till it had been proved and re-proved ten times over, was it understood that the sun could not have stood still upon Gideon. Craswell, who was a member, and who took his seat during these debates without venturing to speak, merely whispered to his neighbour that the heartless greedy fellow was unwilling to wait for the wools of Little Christchurch.

Three divisions were made on the debate, and thrice did the Fixed-Periodists beat the old party by a majority of fifteen in a House consisting of eighty-five members. So strong was the feeling in the empire, that only two members were absent, and the number remained the same during the whole week of the debate. This, I did think, was a triumph;

and I felt that the old country, which had really nothing on earth to do with the matter, could not interfere with an opinion expressed so strongly. My heart throbbed with pleasureable emotion as I heard that old age, which I was myself approaching, depicted in terms which made its impotence truly conspicuous, —till I felt that, had it been proposed to deposit all of us who had reached the age of fifty-eight, I really think that I should joyfully have given my assent to such a measure, and have walked off at once and deposited myself in the college.

But it was only at such moments that I was allowed to experience this feeling of triumph. I was encountered not only in my own house but in society generally, and on the very streets of Gladstonopolis, by the expression of an opinion that Crasweller would not be made to retire to the college at his Fixed Period. " What on earth is there to hinder it ? " I said once to my old friend Ruggles. Ruggles was now somewhat over sixty, and was an agent in the town for country wool-growers. He took no part in politics; and though he had never agreed to the principle of the Fixed Period, had not interested himself in opposition to it. He was a man whom I regarded as indifferent to length of life, but one who would, upon the whole, rather face such lot as Nature might intend for him, than seek to improve it by any new reform.

"Eva Crasweller will hinder it," said Ruggles.

"Eva is a mere child. Do you suppose that her opinion will be allowed to interrupt the laws of the whole community, and oppose the progress of civilisation?"

"Her feelings will," said Ruggles. "Who's to stand a daughter interceding for the life of her father?"

"One man cannot, but eighty-five can do so."

"The eighty-five will be to the community

just what the one would be to the eighty-five.
I am not saying anything about your law. I
am not expressing an opinion whether it would
be good or bad. I should like to live out my
own time, though I acknowledge that you
Assembly men have on your shoulders the
responsibility of deciding whether I shall do
so or not. You could lead me away and deposit me without any trouble, because I am
not popular. But the people are beginning to
talk about Eva Crasweller and Abraham Grundle, and I tell you that all the volunteers you
have in Britannula will not suffice to take the
old man to the college, and to keep him there
till you have polished him off. He would be
deposited again at Little Christchurch in
triumph, and the college would be left a
wreck behind him."

This view of the case was peculiarly dis-
tressing to me. As the chief magistrate of
the community, nothing is so abhorrent to
me as rebellion. Of a populace that are not

law - abiding, nothing but evil can be pre-
dicted ; whereas a people who will obey the
laws cannot but be prosperous.   It grieved
me greatly to be told that the inhabitants of
Gladstonopolis would rise in tumult and destroy the college merely to favour the views
of a pretty girl.   Was there any honour, or
worse again, could there be any utility, in
being the President of a republic in which
such things could happen?   I left my friend
Ruggles in the street, and passed on to the
executive hall in a very painful frame of
mind.

When there, tidings reached me of a much
sadder nature.   At the very moment at which
I had been talking with Ruggles in the street
on the subject, a meeting had been held in
the market-place with the express purpose of
putting down the Fixed Period ; and who had
been the chief orator on the occasion but Jack
Neverbend!   My own son had taken upon
himself this new work of public speechifying

in direct opposition to his own father! And I had reason to believe that he was instigated to do so by my own wife! "Your son, sir, has been addressing the multitude about the Fixed Period, and they say that it has been quite beautiful to hear him." It was thus that the matter was told me by one of the clerks in my office, and I own that I did receive some slight pleasure at finding that Jack could do something beyond cricket. But it became immediately necessary to take steps to stop the evil, and I was the more bound to do so because the only delinquent named to me was my own son.

"If it be so," I said aloud in the office, "Jack Neverbend shall sleep this night in prison." But it did not occur to me at the moment that it would be necessary I should have formal evidence that Jack was conspiring against the laws before I could send him to jail. I had no more power over him in that respect than on any one else. Had I declared that he should be sent to bed without his supper, I should have expressed myself better both as a father and a magistrate.

I went home, and on entering the house the first person that I saw was Eva. Now, as this matter went on, I became full of wrath with my son, and with my wife, and with poor old Crasweller; but I never could bring myself to be angry with Eva There was a coaxing, sweet, feminine way with her which overcame all opposition. And I had already begun to regard her as my daughter-in-law, and to love her dearly in that position, although there were moments in which Jack's impudence and new spirit of opposition almost tempted me to disinherit him.

"Eva," I said, "what is this that I hear of a public meeting in the streets?"

"Oh, Mr Neverbend," she said, taking me by the arm, "there are only a few boys who are talking about papa." Through all the noises and tumults of these times there was an evident determination to speak of Jack as a boy. Everything that he did and all that he said were merely the efflux of his high spirits as a schoolboy. Eva always spoke of him as a kind of younger brother. And yet I soon found that the one opponent whom I had most to fear in Britannula was my own son.

"But why," I asked, "should these foolish boys discuss the serious question respecting your dear father in the public street?"

"They don't want to have him—deposited," she said, almost sobbing as she spoke.

"But, my dear," I began, determined to teach her the whole theory of the Fixed Period with all its advantages from first to last.

But she interrupted me at once. "Oh, Mr Neverbend, I know what a good thing it is— to talk about. I have no doubt the world will be a great deal the better for it. And if all the papas had been deposited for the last five hundred years, I don't suppose that I should care so much about it. But to be the first that ever it happened to in all the world! Why should papa be the first? You ought to begin with some weak, crotchety, poor old cripple, who would be a great deal better out of the way. But papa is in excellent health, and has all his wits about him a great deal better than Mr Grundle. He manages everything at Little Christchurch, and manages it very well."

"But, my dear——" I was going to explain to her that in a question of such enormous public interest as this of the Fixed Period it was impossible to consider the merits of individual cases. But she interrupted me again before I could get out a word.

"Oh, Mr Neverbend, they'll never be able to do it, and I'm afraid that then you'll be vexed."

"My dear, if the law be——"

"Oh yes, the law is a very beautiful thing; but what's the good of laws if they cannot be carried out? There's Jack there;—of course he is only a boy, but he swears that all the executive, and all the Assembly, and all the volunteers in Britannula, shan't lead my papa into that beastly college"

"Beastly! My dear, you cannot have seen the college. It is perfectly beautiful."

"That's only what Jack says. It's Jack that calls it beastly. Of course he's not much of a man as yet, but he is your own son. And I do think, that for an earnest spirit about a thing, Jack is a very fine fellow."

"Abraham Grundle, you know, is just as warm on the other side."

"I hate Abraham Grundle. I don't want ever to hear his name again. I understand very well what it is that Abraham Grundle is after. He never cared a straw for me; nor I much for him, if you come to that."

"But you are contracted."

"If you think that I am going to marry a man because our names have been written down in a book together, you are very much mistaken. He is a nasty mean fellow, and I will never speak to him again as long as I live. He would deposit papa this very moment if he had the power. Whereas Jack is determined to stand up for him as long as he has got a tongue to shout or hands to fight." These were terrible words, but I had heard the same sentiment myself from Jack's own lips. "Of course Jack is nothing to me," she continued, with that half sob which had become habitual to her whenever she was forced to speak of her father's deposition. "He is only a boy, but we all know that he could thrash Abraham Grundle at once. And to my thinking he is much more fit to be a member of the Assembly."

As she would not hear a word that I said to her, and was only intent on expressing the warmth of her own feelings, I allowed her to go her way, and retired to the privacy of my own library. There I endeavoured to console myself as best I might by thinking of the brilliant nature of Jack's prospects. He himself was over head and ears in love with Eva, and it was clear to me that Eva was nearly as fond of him. And then the sly rogue had found the certain way to obtain old Crasweller's consent. Grundle had thought that if he could once see his father-in-law deposited, he would have nothing to do but to walk into Little Christchurch as master. That was the accusation generally made against him in Gladstonopolis. But Jack, who did not, as far as I could see, care a straw for humanity in the matter, had vehemently taken the side of the Anti-Fixed-Periodists as the safest way to get the father's consent. There was a contract of marriage, no doubt, and Grundle would be entitled to take a quarter of the father's possessions if he could prove that the contract had been broken. Such was the law of Britannula on the subject. But not a shilling had as yet been claimed by any man under that law. And Crasweller no doubt concluded that Grundle would be unwilling to bear the odium of being the first. And there were clauses in the law which would make it very difficult for him to prove the validity of the contract. It had been already asserted by many that a girl could not be expected to marry the man who had endeavoured to destroy her father; and although in my mind there could be no doubt that Abraham Grundle had only done his duty as a senator, there was no knowing what view of the case a jury might take in Gladstonopolis. And then, if the worst came to the worst, Crasweller would resign a fourth of his property almost without a pang, and Jack would content himself in making the meanness of Grundle conspicuous to his fellow-citizens.

And now I must confess that, as I sat alone in my library, I did hesitate for an hour as to my future conduct. Might it not be better for me to abandon altogether the Fixed Period and all its glories? Even in Britannula the

world might be too strong for me. Should
I not take the good things that were offered,
and allow Jack to marry his wife and be
happy in his own way? In my very heart
I loved him quite as well as did his mother,
and thought that he was the finest young
fellow that Britannula had produced. And if
this kind of thing went on, it might be that
I should be driven to quarrel with him altogether, and to have him punished under the
law, like some old Roman of old. And I must
confess that my relations with Mrs Neverbend
made me very unfit to ape the Roman *pater-
familias*. She never interfered with public
business, but she had a way of talking about
household matters in which she was always
victorious. Looking back as I did at this
moment on the past, it seemed to me that she
and Jack, who were the two persons I loved
best in the world, had been the enemies who
had always successfully conspired against me.
"Do have done with your Fixed Period and

nonsense,' she had said to me only yesterday. "It's all very well for the Assembly; but when you come to killing poor Mr Crasweller in real life, it is quite out of the question." And then, when I began to explain to her at length the immense importance of the subject, she only remarked that that would do very well for the Assembly. Should I abandon it all, take the good things with which God had provided me, and retire into private life? I had two sides to my character, and could see myself sitting in luxurious comfort amidst the furniture of Crasweller's verandah while Eva and her children were around. and Jack was standing with a cigar in his mouth outside laying down the law for the cricketers at Gladstonopolis. "Were not better done as others use," I said to myself over and over again as I sat there wearied with this contest, and thinking of the much more frightful agony I should be called upon to endure when the time had actually come for the departure of old Crasweller.

And then again if I should fail! For half
an hour or so I did fear that I should fail. I
had been always a most popular magistrate,
but now, it seemed, had come the time in
which all my popularity must be abandoned.
Jack, who was quick enough at understanding
the aspect of things, had already begun to ask
the people whether they would see their old
friend Crasweller murdered in cold blood. It
was a dreadful word, but I was assured that
he had used it. How would it be when the
time even for depositing had come, and an
attempt was made to lead the old man up
through the streets of Gladstonopolis? Should
I have strength of character to perform the
task in opposition to the loudly expressed
wishes of the inhabitants, and to march him
along protected by a strong body of volunteers?
And how would it be if the volunteers themselves refused to act on the side of law and
order? Should I not absolutely fail; and
would it not afterwards be told of me that,

as President, I had broken down in an attempt to carry out the project with which my name had been so long associated?

As I sat there alone I had almost determined to yield. But suddenly there came upon me a memory of Socrates, of Galileo, of Hampden, and of Washington. What great things had these men done by constancy, in opposition to the wills and prejudices of the outside world! How triumphant they now appeared to have been in fighting against the enormous odds which power had brought against them! And how pleasant now were the very sounds of their names to all who loved their fellow-creatures! In some moments of private thought, anxious as were now my own, they too must have doubted. They must have asked themselves the question, whether they were strong enough to carry their great re-forms against the world. But in these very moments the necessary strength had been given to them. It must have been that, when almost despairing, they had been comforted by an inner truth, and had been all but inspired to trust with confidence in their cause. They, too, had been weak, and had trembled, and had almost feared. But they had found in their own hearts that on which they could rely. Had they been less sorely pressed than was I now at this present moment? Had not they believed and trusted and been confident? As I thought of it, I became aware that it was not only necessary for a man to imagine new truths, but to be able to endure, and to suffer, and to bring them to maturity. And how often before a truth was brought to maturity must it be necessary that he who had imagined it, and seen it, and planned it, must give his very life for it, and all in vain? But not perhaps all in vain as far as the world was concerned; but only in vain in regard to the feelings and knowledge of the man himself. In struggling for the welfare of his fellow-creatures, a man must dare to endure to be obliterated, — must be content to go down unheard of, — or, worse still, ridiculed, and perhaps abused by all, — in order that something afterwards may remain of those changes which he has been enabled to see, but not to carry out. How many things are requisite to true greatness! But, first of all, is required that self-negation which is able to plan new blessings, although certain that those blessings will be accounted as curses by the world at large.

Then I got up, and as I walked about the room I declared to myself aloud my purpose. Though I might perish in the attempt, I would certainly endeavour to carry out the doctrine of the Fixed Period. Though the people might be against me, and regard me as their enemy, —that people for whose welfare I had done it all, — still I would persevere, even though I might be destined to fall in the attempt. Though the wife of my bosom and the son of my loins should turn against me, and embitter my last moments by their enmity, still would I persevere. When they came to speak of the vices and the virtues of President Neverbend,—to tell of his weakness and his strength,—it should never be said of him that he had been deterred by fear of the people from carrying out the great measure which he had projected solely for their benefit.

Comforted by this resolve, I went into Mrs Neverbend's parlour, where I found her son Jack sitting with her. They had evidently been talking about Jack's speech in the market-place; and I could see that the young orator's brow was still flushed with the triumph of the moment. "Father," said he, immediately, "you will never be able to deposit old Crasweller. People won't let you do it."

"The people of Britannula," I said, "will never interfere to prevent their magistrate from acting in accordance with the law."

"Bother!" said Mrs Neverbend. When my wife said "bother," it was, I was aware, of no use to argue with her. Indeed, Mrs Neverbend is a lady upon whom argument is for the most part thrown away. She forms her opinion from the things around her, and is, in regard to domestic life, and to her neighbours, and to the conduct of people with whom she lives, almost invariably right. She has a quick insight, and an affectionate heart, which together keep her from going astray. She knows how to do good, and when to do it. But to abstract argument, and to political truth, she is wilfully blind. I felt it to be necessary that I should select this opportunity for making Jack understand that I would not fear his opposition; but I own that I could have wished that Mrs Neverbend had not been present on the occasion.

"Won't they?" said Jack. "That's just what I fancy they will do."

"Do you mean to say that it is what you wish them to do,—that you think it right that they should do it?"

"I don't think Crasweller ought to be deposited, if you mean that, father."

"Not though the law requires it?" This I said in a tone of authority. "Have you formed any idea in your own mind of the subjection to the law which is demanded from all good citizens? Have you ever bethought yourself that the law should be in all things——"

"Oh, Mr President, pray do not make a speech here," said my wife. "I shall never understand it, and I do not think that Jack is much wiser than I am."

"I do not know what you mean by a speech, Sarah." My wife's name is Sarah. "But it is necessary that Jack should be instructed that he, at any rate, must obey the law. He is my son, and, as such, it is essentially necessary that he should be amenable to it. The law demands——"

"You can't do it, and there's an end of it," said Mrs Neverbend. "You and all your laws will never be able to put an end to poor Mr

Crasweller,—and it would be a great shame if you did. You don't see it; but the feeling here in the city is becoming very strong. The people won't have it; and I must say that it is only rational that Jack should be on the same side. He is a man now, and has a right to his own opinion as well as another."

"Jack," said I, with much solemnity, "do you value your father's blessing?"

"Well; sir, yes," said he. "A blessing, I suppose, means something of an allowance paid quarterly."

I turned away my face that he might not see the smile which I felt was involuntarily creeping across it. "Sir," said I, "a father's blessing has much more than a pecuniary value. It includes that kind of relation between a parent and his son without which life would be a burden to me, and, I should think, very grievous to you also."

"Of course I hope that you and I may always be on good terms."

I was obliged to take this admission for what it was worth. "If you wish to remain on good terms with me," said I, "you must not oppose me in public when I am acting as a public magistrate."

"Is he to see Mr Crasweller murdered before his very eyes, and to say nothing about it?" said Mrs Neverbend.

Of all terms in the language there was none so offensive to me as that odious word when used in reference to the ceremony which I had intended to be so gracious and alluring. "Sarah," said I, turning upon her in my anger, "that is a very improper word, and one which you should not tempt the boy to use, especially in my presence."

"English is English, Mr President," she said. She always called me "Mr President" when she intended to oppose me.

"You might as well say that a man was murdered when he is—is—killed in battle." I had been about to say "executed," but I stopped myself. Men are not executed in Britannula.

"No. He is fighting his country's battle and dies gloriously."

"He has his leg shot off, or his arm, and is too frequently left to perish miserably on the ground. Here every comfort will be provided for him, so that he may depart from this world without a pang, when, in the course of years, he shall have lived beyond the period at which he can work and be useful."

"But look at Mr Crasweller, father. Who is more useful than he is?"

Nothing had been more unlucky to me as the promoter of the Fixed Period than the peculiar healthiness and general sanity of him who was by chance to be our first martyr. It might have been possible to make Jack understand that a rule which had been found to be applicable to the world at large was not fitted for some peculiar individual, but it was quite impossible to bring this home to the mind of Mrs Neverbend. I must, I felt, choose some other opportunity for expounding that side of the argument. I would at the present moment take a leaf out of my wife's book and go straight to my purpose "I tell you what it is, young man," said I; "I do not intend to be thwarted by you in carrying on the great reform to which I have devoted my life. If you cannot hold your tongue at the present moment, and abstain from making public addresses in the market-place, you shall go out of Britannula. It is well that you should travel and see something of the world before you commence the trade of public orator. Now I think of it, the Alpine Club from Sydney are to be in New Zealand this summer, and it will suit you very well to go and climb up Mount Earnshawe and see all the beauties of nature instead of talking nonsense here in Gladstonopolis."

"Oh, father, I should like nothing better," cried Jack, enthusiastically.

"Nonsense," said Mrs Neverbend; "are you going to send the poor boy to break his neck among the glaciers? Don't you remember that Dick Ardwinkle was lost there a year or two ago, and came to his death in a most frightful manner?"

"That was before I was born," said Jack, "or at any rate very shortly afterwards And they hadn't then invented the new patent steel climbing arms. Since they came up, no one has ever been lost among the glaciers."

"You had better prepare then to go," said I, thinking that the idea of getting rid of Jack in this manner was very happy.

"But, father," said he, "of course I can't stir a step till after the great cricket-match."

"You must give up cricket for this time So good an opportunity for visiting the New Zealand mountains may never come again."

"Give up the match!" he exclaimed. "Why, the English sixteen are coming here on purpose to play us, and swear that they'll beat us by means of the new catapult. But I know that our steam-bowler will beat their catapult hollow. At any rate I cannot stir from here till after the match is over. I've got to arrange everything myself. Besides, they do count something on my spring-batting. I should be regarded as absolutely a traitor to my country if I were to leave Britannula while this is going on. The young Marquis of Marylebone, their leader, is to stay at our house; and the vessel bringing them will be due here about eleven o'clock next Wednesday."

"Eleven o'clock next Wednesday," said I, in surprise. I had not as yet heard of this match, nor of the coming of our aristocratic visitor.

"They won't be above thirty minutes late at the outside. They left the Land's End three weeks ago last Tuesday at two, and London at half-past ten. We have had three or four water telegrams from them since they started, and they hadn't then lost ten minutes on the journey. Of course I must be at home to receive the Marquis of Marylebone."

All this set me thinking about many things. It was true that at such a moment I could not use my parental authority to send Jack out of the island. To such an extent had the childish amusements of youth been carried, as to give to them all the importance of politics and social science. What I had heard about this cricket-match had gone in at one ear and come out at the other; but now that it was brought home to me, I was aware that all my authority would not serve to banish Jack till it was over. Not only would he not obey me, but he would be supported in his disobedience by even the elders of the community. But perhaps the worst feature of it all was the arrival just now at Gladstonopolis of a crowd of educated Englishmen. When I say educated I mean prejudiced. They would be Englishmen with no ideas beyond those cur-

rent in the last century, and would be altogether deaf to the wisdom of the Fixed Period.
I saw at a glance that I must wait till they
should have taken their departure, and postpone all further discussion on the subject as
far as might be possible till Gladstonopolis
should have been left to her natural quiescence
after the disturbance of the cricket "Very
well," said I, leaving the room. "Then it
may come to pass that you will never be
able to visit the wonderful glories of Mount
Earnshawe."

"Plenty of time for that," said Jack, as I
shut the door

CHAPTER V.

THE CRICKET-MATCH.

I HAD been of late so absorbed in the affairs of the Fixed Period, that I had altogether forgotten the cricket-match and the noble strangers who were about to come to our shores Of course I had heard of it before, and had been informed that Lord Marylebone was to be our guest. I had probably also been told that Sir Lords Longstop and Sir Kennington Oval were to be entertained at Little Christchurch. But when I was reminded of this by Jack a few days later, it had quite gone out of my head. But I now at once began to recognise the importance of the occasion, and to see that for the next two months Crasweller, the college,

and the Fixed Period must be banished, if not
from my thoughts, at any rate from my tongue.
Better could not be done in the matter than
to have them banished from the tongue of all
the world, as I certainly should not be anxious
to have the subject ventilated within hearing
and speaking of the crowd of thoroughly old-
fashioned, prejudiced, aristocratic young Englishmen who were coming to us.   The cricket-
match sprang to the front so suddenly, that
Jack seemed to have forgotten all his energy
respecting the college, and to have transferred
his entire attention to the various weapons,
offensive and defensive, wherewith the London
club was, if possible, to be beaten.   We are
never short of money in Britannula; but it
seemed, as I watched the various preparations
made for carrying on two or three days' play
at Little Christchurch, that England must be
sending out another army to take another
Sebastopol.   More paraphernalia were required
to enable these thirty-two lads to play their

game with propriety than would have been
needed for the depositing of half Gladstonopolis. Every man from England had his
attendant to look after his bats and balls, and
shoes and greaves; and it was necessary, of
course, that our boys should be equally well
served. Each of them had two bicycles for his
own use, and as they were all constructed with
the new double-acting levers, they passed backwards and forwards along the bicycle track
between the city and Crasweller's house with
astonishing rapidity. I used to hear that the
six miles had been done in fifteen minutes.
Then there came a struggle with the English
and the Britannulists, as to which would get
the nearest to fourteen minutes; till it seemed
that bicycle-racing and not cricket had been
the purpose for which the English had sent
out the 4000-ton steam-yacht at the expense
of all the cricketers of the nation. It was on
this occasion that the track was first divided
for comers and goers, and that volunteers were

set to prevent stragglers from crossing except by the regular bridges. I found that I, the President of the Republic, was actually forbidden to go down in my tricycle to my old friend's house, unless I would do so before noon. "You'd be run over and made mincemeat of," said Jack, speaking of such a catastrophe with less horror than I thought it ought to have engendered in his youthful mind. Poor Sir Lords was run down by our Jack, —collided as Jack called it. "He hadn't quite impetus enough on to make the turning sharp as he ought," said Jack, without the slightest apparent regret at what had occurred. "Another inch and a half would have saved him. If he can touch a ball from our steam-bowler when I send it, I shall think more of his arms than I do of his legs, and more of his eyes than I do of his lungs. What a fellow to send out! Why, he's thirty, and has been eating soup, they tell me, all through the journey." These young men had brought a doctor with them,

Dr MacNuffery, to prescribe to them what to eat and drink at each meal; and the unfortunate baronet whom Jack had nearly slaughtered, had encountered the ill-will of the entire club because he had called for mutton-broth when he was sea-sick.

They were to be a month in Britannula before they would begin the match, so necessary was it that each man should be in the best possible physical condition. They had brought their Dr MacNuffery, and our lads immediately found the need of having a doctor of their own. There was, I think, a little pretence in this, as though Dr Bobbs had been a long-established officer of the Southern Cross cricket club, they had not in truth thought of it, and Bobbs was only appointed the night after MacNuffery's position and duties had been made known. Bobbs was a young man just getting into practice in Gladstonopolis, and understood measles, I fancy, better than the training of athletes. MacNuffery was the most disagree-

able man of the English party, and soon began
to turn up his nose at Bobbs. But Bobbs, I
think, got the better of him. "Do you allow
coffee to your club;—coffee?" asked MacNuffery,
in a voice mingling ridicule and reproof with
a touch of satire, as he had begun to guess
that Bobbs had not been long attending to his
present work. "You'll find," said Bobbs, "that
young men in our air do not need the restraints
which are necessary to you English. Their
fathers and mothers were not soft and flabby
before them, as was the case with yours, I
think." Lord Marylebone looked across the
table, I am told, at Sir Kennington Oval, and
nothing afterwards was said about diet.

But a great trouble arose, which, however,
rather assisted Jack in his own prospects in
the long-run,—though for a time it seemed to
have another effect. Sir Kennington Oval was
much struck by Eva's beauty, and, living as he
did in Crasweller's house, soon had an opportunity of so telling her. Abraham Grundle

was one of the cricketers, and, as such, was frequently on the ground at Little Christchurch; but he did not at present go into Crasweller's house, and the whole fashionable community of Gladstonoplis was beginning to entertain the opinion that that match was off. Grundle had been heard to declare most authoritatively that when the day came Crasweller should be deposited, and had given it as his opinion that the power did not exist which could withstand the law of Britannula. Whether in this he preferred the law to Eva, or acted in anger against Crasweller for interfering with his prospects, or had an idea that it would not be worth his while to marry the girl while the girl's father should be left alive, or had gradually fallen into this bitterness of spirit from the opposition shown to him, I could not quite tell. And he was quite as hostile to Jack as to Crasweller. But he seemed to entertain no aversion at all to Sir Kennington Oval; nor, I was informed, did Eva. I had known that for the last month Jack's mother had been instant with him to induce him to speak out to Eva; but he, who hardly allowed me, his father, to open my mouth without contradicting me, and who in our house ordered everything about just as though he were the master, was so bashful in the girl's presence that he had never as yet asked her to be his wife. Now Sir Kennington had come in his way, and he by no means carried his modesty so far as to abstain from quarrelling with him. Sir Kennington was a good-looking young aristocrat, with plenty of words, but nothing special to say for himself. He was conspicuous for his cricketing finery, and when got up to take his place at the wicket, looked like a diver with his diving-armour all on; but Jack said that he was very little good at the game. Indeed, for mere cricket Jack swore that the English would be "nowhere" but for eight professional players whom they had brought out with them. It must be explained that our club had no professionals. We had not come to that yet, —that a man should earn his bread by playing cricket. Lord Marylebone and his friend had brought with them eight professional "slaves," as our young men came to call them,—most ungraciously. But each "slave" required as much looking after as did the masters, and they thought a great deal more of themselves than did the non-professionals.

Jack had in truth been attempting to pass Sir Kennington on the bicycle track when he had upset poor Sir Lords Longstop; and, according to his own showing, he had more than once allowed Sir Kennington to start in advance, and had run into Little Christchurch bicycle quay before him. This had not given rise to the best feeling, and I feared lest there might be an absolute quarrel before the match should have been played. "I'll punch that fellow's head some of these days," Jack said one evening when he came back from Little Christchurch.

"What's the matter now?" I asked.

"Impudent puppy! He thinks because he has got an unmeaning handle to his name, that everybody is to come to his whistle. They tell me that his father was made what they call a baronet because he set a broken arm for one of those twenty royal dukes that England has to pay for."

"Who has had to come to his whistle now?" asked his mother.

"He went over with his steam curricle, and sent to ask Eva whether she would not take a drive with him on the cliffs."

"She needn't have gone unless she wished it," I said.

"But she did go; and there she was with him for a couple of hours. He's the most unmeaning upstart of a puppy I ever met. He has not three ideas in the world. I shall tell Eva what I think about him."

The quarrel went on during the whole period of preparation, till it seemed as though Glad-

stonopolis had nothing else to talk about.
Eva's name was in every one's mouth, till my
wife was nearly beside herself with anger. "A
girl," said she, "shouldn't get herself talked
about in that way by every one all round. I
don't suppose the man intends to marry her."

"I can't see why he shouldn't," I replied.

"She's nothing more to him than a pretty
provincial lass. What would she be in London?"

"Why should not Mr Crasweller's daughter
be as much admired in London as here?" I
answered. "Beauty is the same all the world
over, and her money will be thought of quite
as much there as here."

"But she will have such a spot upon her."

"Spot! What spot?"

"As the daughter of the first deposited of
the Fixed Period people,—if ever that comes
off. Or if it don't, she'll be talked about as
her who was to be. I don't suppose any Englishman will think of marrying her."

This made me very angry. "What!" I said. "Do you, a Britannulist and my wife, intend to turn the special glory of Britannula to the disgrace of her people? That which we should be ready to claim as the highest honour,—as being an advance in progress and general civilisation never hitherto even thought of among other people,—to have conceived that, and to have prepared it, in every detail for perfect consummation,—that is to be accounted as an opprobrium to our children, by you, the Lady President of the Republic! Have you no love of country, no patriotism, no feeling at any rate of what has been done for the world's welfare by your own family?" I own I did feel vexed when she spoke of Eva as having been as it were contaminated by being a Britannulist, because of the law enacting the Fixed Period.

"She'd better face it out at home than go across the world to hear what other people say of us. It may be all very well as far as state wisdom goes; but the world isn't ripe for it, and we shall only be laughed at."

There was truth in this, and a certain amount of concession had also been made. I can fancy that an easy-going butterfly should laugh at the painful industry of the ant; and I should think much of the butterfly who should own that he was only a butterfly because it was the age of butterflies. "The few wise," said I, "have ever been the laughing-stock of silly crowds."

"But Eva isn't one of the wise," she replied, "and would be laughed at without having any of your philosophy to support her. However, I don't suppose the man is thinking of it."

But the young man was thinking of it; and had so far made up his mind before he went as to ask Eva to marry him out of hand and return with him to England. We heard of it when the time came, and heard also that Eva had declared that she could not make up her mind so quickly. That was what was said when the time drew near for the departure of the yacht. But we did not hear it direct from Eva, nor yet from Crasweller. All these tidings came to us from Jack, and Jack was in this instance somewhat led astray.

Time passed on, and the practice on the little Christchurch ground was continued. Several accidents happened, but the cricketers took very little account of these. Jack had his cheek cut open by a ball running off his bat on to his face; and Eva, who saw the accident, was carried fainting into the house. Sir Kennington behaved admirably, and himself brought him home in his curricle. We were told afterwards that this was done at Eva's directions, because old Crasweller would have been uncomfortable with the boy in his house, seeing that he could not in his present circumstances receive me or my wife. Mrs Neverbend swore a solemn oath that Jack should be made to abandon his cricket; but Jack was playing again the next day, with his face strapped up

athwart and across with republican black-silk
adhesive. When I saw Bobbs at work over
him I thought that one side of his face was
gone, and that his eye would be dreadfully
out of place. "All his chance of marrying
Eva is gone," said I to my wife. "The nasty
little selfish slut!" said Mrs Neverbend. But
at two the next day Jack had been patched
up, and nothing could keep him from Little
Christchurch. Bobbs was with him the whole
morning, and assured his mother that if he
could go out and take exercise his eye would
be all right. His mother offered to take a
walk with him in the city park, but Bobbs
declared that violent exercise would be necessary to keep the eye in its right place, and
Jack was at Little Christchurch manipulating
his steam-bowler in the afternoon. Afterwards
Littlebat, one of the English professionals, had
his leg broken, and was necessarily laid on
one side; and young Grundle was hurt on
the lower part of the back, and never showed

himself again on the scene of danger. "My life is too precious in the Assembly just at present," he said to me, excusing himself. He alluded to the Fixed Period debate, which he knew would be renewed as soon as the cricketers were gone. I no doubt depended very much on Abraham Grundle, and assented. The match was afterwards carried on with fifteen on each side; for though each party had spare players, they could not agree as to the use of them. Our next man was better than theirs, they said, and they were anxious that we should take our second best, to which our men would not agree. Therefore the game was ultimately played with thirty combatants.

"So one of our lot is to come back for a wife almost immediately," said Lord Marylebone at our table the day before the match was to be played. .

"Oh, indeed, my lord!" said Mrs Neverbend. "I am glad to find that a Britannulan young lady has been so effective. Who is the gentleman?" It was easy to see by my wife's face, and to know by her tone of voice, that she was much disturbed by the news.

"Sir Kennington," said Lord Marylebone. "I supposed you had all heard of it." Of course we had all heard of it; but Lord Marylebone did not know what had been Mrs Neverbend's wishes for her own son.

"We did know that Sir Kennington had been very attentive, but there is no knowing what that means from you foreign gentlemen. It's a pity that poor Eva, who is a good girl in her way, should have her head turned." This came from my wife.

"It's Oval's head that is turned," continued his lordship; "I never saw a man so bowled over in my life. He's awfully in love with her."

"What will his friends say at home?" asked Mrs Neverbend.

"We understand that Miss Crasweller is to have a large fortune; eight or ten thousand a-year at the least. I should imagine that she will be received with open arms by all the Ovals; and as for a foreigner,—we don't call you foreigners."

"Why not?" said I, rather anxious to prove that we were foreigners. "What makes a foreigner but a different allegiance? Do we not call the Americans foreigners?" Great Britain and France had been for years engaged in the great maritime contest with the united fleets of Russia and America, and had only just made that glorious peace by which, as politicians said, all the world was to be governed for the future; and after that, it need not be doubted but that the Americans were foreign to the English;—and if the Americans, why not the Britannulists? We had separated ourselves from Great Britain, without coming to blows indeed; but still our own flag, the Southern Cross, flew as proudly to our gentle breezes as ever had done the Union-jack amidst the inclemency of a British winter. It was the flag of Britannula, with which Great Britain had no concern. At the present moment I was specially anxious to hear a distinguished Englishman like Lord Marylebone acknowledge that we were foreigners "If we be not foreigners, what are we, my lord?"

"Englishmen, of course," said he. "What else? Don't you talk English?"

"So do the Americans, my lord," said I, with a smile that was intended to be gracious. "Our language is spreading itself over the world, and is no sign of nationality."

"What laws do you obey?"

"English,—till we choose to repeal them You are aware that we have already freed ourselves from the stain of capital punishment."

"Those coins pass in your market-places?" Then he brought out a gold piece from his waistcoat-pocket, and slapped it down on the table. It was one of those pounds which the people will continue to call sovereigns, although the name has been made actually illegal for the rendering of all accounts. "Whose is this image and superscription?" he asked. "And yet this was paid to me to-day at one of your banks, and the lady cashier asked me whether I would take sovereigns. How will you get over that, Mr President?"

A small people,—numerically small,—cannot of course do everything at once. We have been a little slack perhaps in instituting a national mint. In fact there was a difficulty about the utensil by which we would have clapped a Southern Cross over the British arms, and put the portrait of the Britannulan President of the day,—mine for instance,—in the place where the face of the British monarch has hitherto held its own. I have never pushed the question much, lest I should seem, as have done some presidents, over anxious to exhibit myself. I have ever thought more of the glory of our race than of putting forward my own individual self,—as may be seen by the whole history of the college. "I will not attempt to get over it," I said; "but according to my ideas, a nation does not depend on the small external accidents of its coin or its language."

"But on the flag which it flies. After all, a bit of bunting is easy."

"Nor on its flag, Lord Marylebone, but on the hearts of its people. We separated from the old mother country with no quarrel, with no ill-will; but with the mutual friendly wishes of both. If there be a trace of the feeling of antagonism in the word foreigners, I will not use it; but British subjects we are not, and never can be again." This I said because I felt that there was creeping up, as it were in the very atmosphere, a feeling that England should be again asked to annex us, so as to save our old people from the wise decision to which our own Assembly had come. Oh for an adamantine law to protect the human race from the imbecility, the weakness, the discontent, and the extravagance of old age! Lord Marylebone, who saw that I was in earnest, and who was the most courteous of gentlemen, changed the conversation. I had already observed that he never spoke about the Fixed Period in our house, though, in the condition in which the community then was, he must have heard it discussed elsewhere.

The day for the match had come. Jack's face was so nearly healed that Mrs Neverbend had been brought to believe entirely in the efficacy of violent exercise for cuts and bruises. Grundle's back was still bad, and the poor fellow with the broken leg could only be wheeled out in front of the verandah to look at the proceedings through one of those wonderful little glasses which enable the critic to see every motion of the players at half-a-mile's distance. He assured me that the precision with which Jack set his steam-bowler was equal to that of one of those

Shoeburyness gunners who can hit a sparrow as far as they can see him, on condition only that they know the precise age of the bird. I gave Jack great credit in my own mind, because I felt that at the moment he was much down at heart. On the preceding day Sir Kennington had been driving Eva about in his curricle, and Jack had returned home tearing his hair "They do it on purpose to put him off his play," said his mother. But if so, they hadn't known Jack. Nor indeed had I quite known him up to this time.

I was bound myself to see the game, because a special tent and a special glass had been prepared for the President. Crasweller walked by as I took my place, but he only shook his head sadly and was silent. It now wanted but four months to his deposition. Though there was a strong party in his favour, I do not know that he meddled much with it. I did hear from different sources that he still continued to assert that he was only nine years my senior, by which he intended to gain the favour of a postponement of his term by twelve poor months; but I do not think that he ever lent himself to the other party. Under my auspices he had always voted for the Fixed Period, and he could hardly oppose it now in theory. They tossed for the first innings, and the English club won it. It was all England against Britannula! Think of the population of the two countries. We had, however, been taught to believe that no community ever played cricket as did the Britannulans. The English went in first, with the two baronets at the wickets. They looked like two stout Minervas with huge wicker helmets. I know a picture of the goddess, all helmet, spear, and petticoats, carrying her spear over her shoulder as she flies through the air over the cities of the earth. Sir Kennington did not fly, but in other respects he was very like the goddess, so completely enveloped was he in his india-rubber guards, and so wonderful was the machine upon his head, by which his brain and features were to be protected.

As he took his place upon the ground there was great cheering. Then the steam - bowler was ridden into its place by the attendant engineer, and Jack began his work. I could see the colour come and go in his face as he carefully placed the ball and peeped down to get its bearing. It seemed to me as though he were taking infinite care to level it straight and even at Sir Kennington's head. I was told afterwards that he never looked at Sir Kennington, but that, having calculated his distance by means of a quicksilver levelling-glass, his object was to throw the ball on a certain inch of turf, from which it might shoot into the wicket at such a degree as to make it very difficult for Sir Kennington to know what to do with it. It seemed to me to take a long time, during which the fourteen men around all looked as though each man were intending to hop off to some other spot than that on which he was standing. There used, I am told, to be only eleven of these men; but now, in a great match, the long-offs, and the long-ons, and the rest of them, are all doubled. The double long-off was at such a distance that, he being a small man, I could only just see him through the field-glass which I kept in my waistcoat-pocket. When I had been looking hard at them for what seemed to be a quarter of an hour, and the men were apparently becoming tired of their continual hop, and when Jack had stooped and kneeled and sprawled, with one eye shut, in every conceivable attitude, on a sudden there came a sharp snap, a little smoke, and lo, Sir Kennington Oval was——out!

There was no doubt about it I myself saw the two bails fly away into infinite space, and at once there was a sound of kettle-drums, trumpets, fifes, and clarionets. It seemed as though all the loud music of the town band had struck up at the moment with their shrillest notes And a huge gun was let off.

" And let the kettle to the trumpet speak,
The trumpet to the cannoneer without,
The cannons to the heavens, the heavens to earth.
Now drinks the king to Hamlet "

I could not but fancy, at these great signs of success, that I was Hamlet's father.

Sir Kennington Oval was out,—out at the very first ball. There could be no doubt about it, and Jack's triumph was complete. It was melancholy to see the English Minerva, as he again shouldered his spear and walked back to his tent. In spite of Jack's good play, and the success on the part of my own countrymen, I could not but be sorry to think that the young baronet had come half round the world to be put out at the first ball. There was a cruelty in it,—an inhospitality,—which, in spite of the exigencies of the game, went against the grain. Then, when the shouting, and the holloaing, and the flinging up of the ball were still going on, I remembered that, after it, he would have his consolation with Eva. And poor Jack, when his short triumph was over, would have to reflect that, though fortunate in his cricket, he was unhappy in his love. As this occurred to me, I looked back towards the house, and there, from a little lattice window at the end of the verandah, I saw a lady's handkerchief waving. Could it be that Eva was waving it so as to comfort her vanquished British lover? In the meantime Minerva went to his tent, and hid himself among sympathetic friends; and I was told afterwards that he was allowed half a pint of bitter beer by Dr MacNuffery.

After twenty minutes spent in what seemed to me the very ostentation of success, another man was got to the wickets. This was Stumps, one of the professionals, who was not quite so much like a Minerva, though he, too, was prodigiously greaved. Jack again set his ball, snap went the machine, and Stumps wriggled his bat. He touched the ball, and away it flew behind the wicket. Five republican Minervas ran after it as fast as their legs could carry them; and I was told by a gentleman who sat next to me scoring, that a dozen runs had been made He spent a great deal of time in explaining how, in the old times, more than six at a time were never scored. Now all this was altered. A slight tip counted ever so much more than a good forward blow, because the ball went behind the wicket Up flew on all sides of the ground figures to show that Stumps had made a dozen, and two British clarionets were blown with a great deal of vigour. Stumps was a thick-set, solid, solemn-looking man, who had been ridiculed by our side as being much too old for the game; but he seemed to think very little of Jack's precise machine. He kept chopping at the ball, which always went behind, till he had made a great score. It was two hours before Jack had sorely lamed him in the hip, and the umpire had given it leg-before-wicket. Indeed it was leg-before-wicket, as the poor man felt when he was assisted back to his tent. However, he had scored 150. Sir Lords Longstop, too, had run up a good score before he was caught out by the middle long-off,—a marvellous catch they all said it was,—and our trumpets were blown for fully five minutes. But the big gun was only fired when a ball was hurled from the machine directly into the wicket.

At the end of three days the Britishers were all out, and the runs were numbered in four figures. I had my doubts, as I looked at the contest, whether any of them would be left to play out the match. I was informed that I was expected to take the President's seat every day; but when I heard that there were to be two innings for each set, I positively declined. But Crasweller took my place; and I was told that a gleam of joy shot across his worn, sorrowful face when Sir Kennington began the second innings with ten runs. Could he really wish, in his condition, to send his daughter away to England simply that she might be a baronet's wife?

When the Britannulists went in for the
second time, they had 1500 runs to get; and
it was said afterwards that Grundle had bet
four to one against his own side   This was
thought to be very shabby on his part, though
if such was the betting, I don't see why he
should lose his money by backing his friends
Jack declared in my hearing that he would
not put a shilling on.   He did not wish either
to lose his money or to bet against himself
But he was considerably disheartened when
he told me that he was not going in on the
first day of their second innings.   He had
not done much when the Britannulists were
in before,—had only made some thirty or forty
runs; and, worse than that, Sir Kennington
Oval had scored up to 300.   They told me
that his Pallas helmet was shaken with tremendous energy as he made his running.   And
again, that man Stumps had seemed to be
invincible, though still lame, and had carried
out his bat with a tremendous score.   He

trudged away without any sign of triumph; but Jack said that the professional was the best man they had.

On the second day of our party's second innings,—the last day but one of the match, —Jack went in. They had only made 150 runs on the previous day, and three wickets were down. Our kettle-drums had had but little opportunity for making themselves heard. Jack was very despondent, and had had some tiff with Eva. He had asked Eva whether she were not going to England, and Eva had said that perhaps she might do so if some Britannulists did not do their duty. Jack had chosen to take this as a bit of genuine impertinence, and had been very sore about it. Stumps was bowling from the British cata-pult, and very nearly gave Jack his quietus during the first over. He hit wildly, and four balls passed him without touching his wicket. Then came his turn again, and he caught the first ball with his Neverbend

spring-bat,—for he had invented it himself,—
such a swipe, as he called it, that nobody has
ever yet been able to find the ball. The story
goes that it went right up to the verandah,
and that Eva picked it up, and has treasured
it ever since.

Be that as it may, during the whole of that
day, and the next, nobody was able to get him
out. There was a continual banging of the
kettle - drum, which seemed to give him renewed spirits. Every ball as it came to him
was sent away into infinite space. All the
Englishmen were made to retire to further
distances from the wickets, and to stand about
almost at the extremity of the ground. The
management of the catapults was intrusted to
one man after another,—but in vain. Then
they sent the catapults away, and tried the
old-fashioned slow bowling. It was all the
same to Jack. He would not be tempted out
of his ground, but stood there awaiting the
ball, let it come ever so slowly. Through the

first of the two days he stood before his wicket, hitting to the right and the left, till hope seemed to spring up again in the bosom of the Britannulists. And I could see that the Englishmen were becoming nervous and un- easy, although the odds were still much in their favour.

At the end of the first day Jack had scored above 500 ; — but eleven wickets had gone down, and only three of the most inferior players were left to stand up with him. It was considered that Jack must still make another 500 before the game would be won. This would allow only twenty each to the other three players. "But," said Eva to me that evening, "they'll never get the twenty each."

"And on which side are you, Eva?" I inquired with a smile. For in truth I did believe at that moment that she was engaged to the baronet.

"How dare you ask, Mr Neverbend?" she

demanded, with indignation. "Am not I a
Britannulist as well as you?" And as she
walked away I could see that there was a
tear in her eye.

On the last day feelings were carried to a
pitch which was more befitting the last battle
of a great war,—some Waterloo of other ages,
—than the finishing of a prolonged game of
cricket. Men looked, and moved, and talked
as though their all were at stake. I cannot say
that the Englishmen seemed to hate us, or we
them; but that the affair was too serious to
admit of playful words between the parties
And those unfortunates who had to stand up
with Jack were so afraid of themselves that
they were like young country orators about
to make their first speeches. Jack was silent,
determined, and yet inwardly proud of himself,
feeling that the whole future success of the
republic was on his shoulders. He ordered
himself to be called at a certain hour, and
the assistants in our household listened to his

words as though feeling that everything depended on their obedience. He would not go out on his bicycle, as fearing that some accident might occur. "Although, ought I not to wish that I might be struck dead?" he said; "as then all the world would know that though beaten, it had been by the hand of God, and not by our default." It astonished me to find that the boy was quite as eager about his cricket as I was about my Fixed Period.

At eleven o'clock I was in my seat, and on looking round, I could see that all the rank and fashion of Britannula were at the ground. But all the rank and fashion were there for nothing, unless they had come armed with glasses. The spaces required by the cricketers were so enormous that otherwise they could not see anything of the play. Under my canopy there was room for five, of which I was supposed to be able to fill the middle thrones. On the two others sat those who officially scored the game. One seat had been

demanded for Mrs Neverbend. " I will see
his fate,—whether it be his glory or his fall,"
—said his mother, with true Roman feeling.
For the other Eva had asked, and of course
it had been awarded to her. When the play
began, Sir Kennington was at the catapult and
Jack at the opposite wicket, and I could hardly
say for which she felt the extreme interest
which she certainly did exhibit. I, as the day
went on, found myself worked up to such ex-
citement that I could hardly keep my hat on
my head or behave myself with becoming pres-
idential dignity. At one period, as I shall
have to tell, I altogether disgraced myself.

There seemed to be an opinion that Jack
would either show himself at once unequal to
the occasion, and immediately be put out,—
which opinion I think that all Gladstonopolis
was inclined to hold,—or else that he would
get his "eye in" as he called it, and go on as
long as the three others could keep their bats.
I know that his own opinion was the same as

that general in the city, and I feared that his very caution at the outset would be detrimental to him. The great object on our side was that Jack should, as nearly as possible, be always opposite to the bowler. He was to take the four first balls, making but one run off the last, and then beginning another over at the opposite end do the same thing again. It was impossible to manage this exactly; but something might be done towards effecting it. There were the three men with whom to work during the day. The first unfortunately was soon made to retire; but Jack, who had walked up to my chair during the time allowed for fetching down the next man, told me that he had "got his eye," and I could see a settled look of fixed purpose in his face. He bowed most gracefully to Eva, who was so stirred by emotion that she could not allow herself to speak a word. "Oh Jack, I pray for you; I pray for you," said his mother. Jack, I fancy, thought more of Eva's silence than of his mother's prayer.

Jack went back to his place, and hit the first ball with such energy that he drove it into the other stumps and smashed them to pieces. Everybody declared that such a thing had never been before achieved at cricket,—and the ball passed on, and eight or ten runs were scored. After that Jack seemed to be mad with cricketing power. He took off his greaves, declaring that they impeded his running, and threw away altogether his helmet. "Oh, Eva, is he not handsome?" said his mother, in ecstasy, hanging across my chair. Eva sat quiet without a sign. It did not become me to say a word, but I did think that he was very handsome;—and I thought also how uncommonly hard it would be to hold him if he should chance to win the game. Let him make what orations he might against the Fixed Period, all Gladstonopolis would follow him if he won this game of cricket for them.

I cannot pretend to describe all the scenes of that day, nor the growing anxiety of the

Englishmen as Jack went on with one hundred after another. He had already scored nearly 1000 when young Grabbe was caught out. Young Grabbe was very popular, because he was so altogether unlike his partner Grundle. He was a fine frank fellow, and was Jack's great friend. "I don't mean to say that he can really play cricket," Jack had said that morning, speaking with great authority; "but he is the best fellow in the world, and will do exactly what you ask him." But he was out now; and Jack, with over 200 still to make, declared that he gave up the battle almost as lost.

"Don't say that, Mr Neverbend," whispered Eva.

"Ah yes; we're gone coons. Even your sympathy cannot bring us round now. If anything could do it that would!"

"In my opinion," continued Eva, "Britannula will never be beaten as long as Mr Neverbend is at the wicket."

"Sir Kennington has been too much for us, I fear," said Jack, with a forced smile, as he retired.

There was now but the one hope left. Mr Brittlereed remained, but he was all. Mr Brittlereed was a gentleman who had advanced nearer to his Fixed Period than any other of the cricketers He was nearly thirty-five years of age, and was regarded by them all as quite an old man. He was supposed to know all the rules of the game, and to be rather quick in keeping the wicket But Jack had declared that morning that he could not hit a ball in a week of Sundays. "He oughtn't to be here," Jack had whispered; "but you know how those things are managed." I did not know how those things were managed, but I was sorry that he should be there, as Jack did not seem to want him.

Mr Brittlereed now went to his wicket, and was bound to receive the first ball. This he did; made one run, whereas he might have made two, and then had to begin the war over. It certainly seemed as though he had done it on purpose. Jack in his passion broke the handle of his spring-bat, and then had half-a-dozen brought to him in order that he might choose another. "It was his favourite bat," said his mother, and buried her face in her handkerchief.

I never understood how it was that Mr Brittlereed lived through that over; but he did live, although he never once touched the ball. Then it came to be Jack's turn, and he at once scored thirty-nine during the over, leaving himself at the proper wicket for re-commencing the operation. I think that this gave him new life. It added, at any rate, new fire to every Britannulist on the ground, and I must say that after that Mr Brittle-reed managed the matter altogether to Jack's satisfaction. Over after over Jack went on, and received every ball that was bowled.

They tried their catapult with single, double, and even treble action. Sir Kennington did his best, flinging the ball with his most tremendous impetus, and then just rolling it up with what seemed to me the most provoking languor. It was all the same to Jack. He had in truth got his "eye in," and as surely as the ball came to him, it was sent away to some most distant part of the ground. The Britishers were mad with dismay as Jack worked his way on through the last hundred. It was piteous to see the exertions which poor Mr Brittlereed made in running backwards and forwards across the ground. They tried, I think, to bustle him by the rapid succession of their bowling. But the only result was that the ball was sent still further off when it reached Jack's wicket. At last, just as every clock upon the ground struck six with that wonderful unanimity which our clocks have attained since they were all regulated by wires from Greenwich, Jack sent a ball flying up into the air, perfectly regardless whether it might be caught or not, knowing well that the one now needed would be scored before it could come down from the heavens into the hands of any Englishman. It did come down, and was caught by Stumps, but by that time Britannula had won her victory. Jack's total score during that innings was 1275. I doubt whether in the annals of cricket any record is made of a better innings than that. Then it was that, with an absence of that presence of mind which the President of a republic should always remember, I took off my hat and flung it into the air.

Jack's triumph would have been complete, only that it was ludicrous to those who could not but think, as I did, of the very little matter as to which the contest had been raised;—just a game of cricket which two sets of boys had been playing, and which should have been regarded as no more than an amusement,—as a pastime, by which to refresh themselves between their work. But they regarded it as though a great national combat had been fought, and the Britannulists looked upon themselves as though they had been victorious against England. It was absurd to see Jack as he was carried back to Gladstonopolis as the hero of the occasion, and to hear him, as he made his speeches at the dinner which was given on the day, and at which he was called upon to take the chair. I was glad to see, however, that he was not quite so glib with his tongue as he had been when addressing the people. He hesitated a good deal, nay, almost broke down, when he gave the health of Sir Kennington Oval and the British sixteen; and I was quite pleased to hear Lord Marylebone declare to his mother that he was "a wonderfully nice boy." I think the English did try to turn it off a little, as though they had only come out there just for the amusement of the voyage. But Grundle, who had now become quite proud of his country, and who lamented loudly that he should have received so severe an injury in preparing for the game, would not let this pass. "My lord," he said, "what is your population?" Lord Marylebone named sixty million. "We are but two hundred and fifty thousand," said Grundle, "and see what we have done." "We are cocks fighting on our own dunghill," said Jack, "and that does make a deal of difference."

But I was told that Jack had spoken a word to Eva in quite a different spirit before he had left Little Christchurch. "After all, Eva, Sir Kennington has not quite trampled us under his feet," he said.

"Who thought that he would?" said Eva. "My heart has never fainted, whatever some others may have done."

CHAPTER VI.

THE COLLEGE.

I WAS surprised to see that Jack, who was so
bold in playing his match, and who had been
so well able to hold his own against the Englishmen,—who had been made a hero, and had
carried off his heroism so well,—should have
been so shamefaced and bashful in regard to
Eva. He was like a silly boy, hardly daring
to look her in the face, instead of the gallant
captain of the band who had triumphed over
all obstacles. But I perceived, though it seemed
that he did not, that she was quite prepared to
give herself to him, and that there was no real
obstacle between him and all the flocks and
herds of Little Christchurch. Not much had

been seen or heard of Grundle during the match, and as far as Eva was concerned, he had succumbed as soon as Sir Kennington Oval had appeared upon the scene. He had thought so much of the English baronet as to have been cowed and quenched by his grandeur. And Sir Kennington himself had, I think, been in earnest before the days of the cricket-match. But I could see now that Eva had merely played him off against Jack, thinking thereby to induce the younger swain to speak his mind. This had made Jack more than ever intent on beating Sir Kennington, but had not as yet had the effect which Eva had intended. "It will all come right," I said to myself, "as soon as these Englishmen have left the island." But then my mind reverted to the Fixed Period, and to the fast-approaching time for Crasweller's deposition. We were now nearly through March, and the thirtieth of June was the day on which he ought to be led to the college. It was my first anxiety to get rid of these Englishmen before the subject should be again ventilated. I own I was anxious that they should not return to their country with their prejudices strengthened by what they might hear at Gladstonopolis. If I could only get them to go before the matter was again debated, it might be that no strong public feeling would be excited in England till it was too late. That was my first desire; but then I was also anxious to get rid of Jack for a short time. The more I thought of Eva and the flocks, the more determined was I not to allow the personal interests of my boy,—and therefore my own,—to clash in any way with the performance of my public duties.

I heard that the Englishmen were not to go till another week had elapsed. A week was necessary to recruit their strength and to enable them to pack up their bats and bicycles. Neither, however, were packed up till the day before they started; for the track down to

Little Christchurch was crowded with them, and they were still practising as though another match were contemplated. I was very glad to have Lord Marylebone as an inmate in our house, but I acknowledge that I was anxious for him to say something as to his departure. "We have been very proud to have you here, my lord," I remarked.

"I cannot say that we are very proud," he replied, "because we have been so awfully licked. Barring that, I never spent a pleasanter two months in my life, and should not be at all unwilling to stay for another. Your mode of life here seems to me to be quite delightful, and we have been thinking so much of our cricket, that I have hardly as yet had a moment to look at your institutions. What is all this about the Fixed Period?" Jack, who was present, put on a serious face, and assumed that air of determination which I was beginning to fear. Mrs Neverbend pursed up her lips, and said nothing; but I knew what was passing through her mind. I managed to turn the conversation, but I was aware that I did it very lamely.

"Jack," I said to my son, "I got a post-card from New Zealand yesterday." The boats had just begun to run between the two islands six days a-week, and as their regular contract pace was twenty - five miles an hour, it was just an easy day's journey.

"What said the post-card?"

"There's plenty of time for Mount Earn-shawe yet. They all say the autumn is the best. The snow is now disappearing in great quantities."

But an old bird is not to be caught with chaff. Jack was determined not to go to the Eastern Alps this year; and indeed, as I found, not to go till this question of the Fixed Period should be settled. I told him that he was a fool. Although he would have been wrong to assist in depositing his father-in-law for the sake of getting the herd and flocks himself, as Grundle would have done, nevertheless he was hardly bound by any feelings of honour or conscience to keep old Crasweller at Little Christchurch in direct opposition to the laws of the land. But all this I could not explain to him, and was obliged simply to take it as a fact that he would not join an Alpine party for Mount Earnshawe this year. As I thought of all this, I almost feared Jack's presence in Gladstonopolis more than that of the young Englishmen.

It was clear, however, that nothing could be done till the Englishmen were gone, and as I had a day at my disposal I determined to walk up to the college and meditate there on the conduct which it would be my duty to follow during the next two months. The college was about five miles from the town, at the side opposite to you as you enter the town from Little Christchurch, and I had some time since made up my mind how, in the bright genial days of our pleasant winter, I would myself accompany Mr Crasweller through the city in an open barouche as I took him to be deposited, through admiring crowds of his fellow-citizens. I had not then thought that he would be a recreant, or that he would be deterred by the fear of departure from enjoying the honours which would be paid to him. But how different now was his frame of mind from that glorious condition to which I had looked forward in my sanguine hopes! Had it been I, I myself, how proud should I have been of my country and its wisdom, had I been led along as a first hero, to anticipate the euthanasia prepared for me! As it was, I hired an inside cab, and hiding myself in the corner, was carried away to the college unseen by any.

The place was called Necropolis. The name had always been distasteful to me, as I had never wished to join with it the feeling of death. Various names had been proposed for the site. Young Grundle had suggested Cre-

mation Hall, because such was the ultimate
end to which the mere husks and hulls of
the citizens were destined.　But there was
something undignified in the sound, — as
though we were talking of a dancing saloon
or a music hall, — and I would have none
of it.　My idea was to give to the mind
some notion of an approach to good things
to come, and I proposed to call the place
" Aditus."　But men said that it was unmeaning, and declared that Britannulists
should never be ashamed to own the truth.
Necropolis sounded well, they said, and ar-
gued that though no actual remains of the
body might be left there, still the tablets
would remain.　Therefore Necropolis it was
called.　I had hoped that a smiling hamlet
might grow up at the gate, inhabited by those
who would administer to the wants of the deposited ; but I had forgot that the deposited
must come first.　The hamlet had not yet
built itself, and round the handsome gates

there was nothing at present but a desert. While land in Britannula was plenty, no one had cared to select ground so near to those awful furnaces by which the mortal clay should be transported into the air. From the gates up to the temple which stood in the middle of the grounds,—that temple in which the last scene of life was to be encountered,—there ran a broad gravel path, which was intended to become a beautiful avenue. It was at present planted alternately with eucalypti and ilexes — the gum-trees for the present generation, and the green-oaks for those to come; but even the gum-trees had not as yet done much to give a furnished appearance to the place. Some had demanded that cedars and yew-trees should be placed there, and I had been at great pains to explain to them that our object should be to make the spot cheerful, rather than sad. Round the temple, at the back of it, were the sets of chambers in which were to live the deposited during their year of probation. Some of these were very handsome, and were made so, no doubt, with a view of alluring the first comers. In preparing wisdom for babes, it is necessary to wrap up its precepts in candied sweets. But, though handsome, they were at present anything but pleasant abodes. Not one of them had as yet been inhabited. As I looked at them, knowing Crasweller as well as I did, I almost ceased to wonder at his timidity. A hero was wanted; but Crasweller was no hero. Then further off, but still in the circle round the temple, there were smaller abodes, less luxurious, but still comfortable, all of which would in a few short years be inhabited,—if the Fixed Period could be carried out in accordance with my project. And foundations had been made for others still smaller,—for a whole township of old men and women, as in the course of the next thirty years they might come hurrying on to find their last abode in the college. I had already selected one, not by any means the finest or the largest, for myself and my wife, in which we might prepare ourselves for the grand departure. But as for Mrs Neverbend, nothing would bring her to set foot within the precincts of the college ground. "Before those next ten years are gone," she would say, "common-sense will have interfered to let folks live out their lives properly." It had been quite useless for me to attempt to make her understand how unfitting was such a speech for the wife of the President of the Republic. My wife's opposition had been an annoyance to me from the first, but I had consoled myself by thinking how impossible it always is to imbue a woman's mind with a logical idea. And though, in all respects of domestic life, Mrs Neverbend is the best of women, even among women she is the most illogical.

I now inspected the buildings in a sad frame of mind, asking myself whether it would ever come to pass that they should be inhabited for their intended purpose. When the Assembly, in compliance with my advice, had first enacted the law of the Fixed Period, a large sum had been voted for these buildings. As the enthusiasm had worn off, men had asked themselves whether the money had not been wasted, and had said that for so small a community the college had been planned on an absurdly grand scale. Still I had gone on, and had watched them as they grew from day to day, and had allowed no shilling to be spared in perfecting them. In my earlier years I had been very successful in the wool trade, and had amassed what men called a large fortune. During the last two or three years I had devoted a great portion of this to the external adornment of the college, not without many words on the matter from Mrs Neverbend. "Jack is to be ruined," she had said, "in order that all the old men and women may be killed artistically." This and other remarks of the kind I was doomed to bear. It was a part of the difficulty which, as a great reformer, I must endure. But now, as I walked mournfully among the disconsolate and half-finished buildings, I could not but ask myself as to the purpose to which my money had been devoted. And I could not but tell myself that if in coming years these tenements should be left tenantless, my country would look back upon me as one who had wasted the produce of her young energies. But again I bethought me of Columbus and Galileo, and swore that I would go on or perish in the attempt.

As these painful thoughts were agitating my mind, a slow decrepit old gentleman came up to me and greeted me as Mr President. He linked his arm familiarly through mine, and remarked that the time seemed to be very long before the college received any of its inhabitants. This was Mr Graybody, the curator, who had been specially appointed to occupy a certain residence, to look after the grounds, and to keep the books of the establishment. Graybody and I had come as young men to Britannula together, and whereas I had succeeded in all my own individual attempts, he had unfortunately failed. He was exactly of my age, as was also his wife. But under the stress of misfortune they had both become unnaturally old, and had at last been left ruined and hopeless, without a shilling on which to depend. I had always been a sincere friend to Graybody, though he was, indeed, a man very difficult to befriend. On most subjects he thought as I did, if he can be said to have thought at all. At any rate he had agreed with me as to the Fixed Period, saying how good it would be if he could be deposited at fifty-eight, and had always declared how blessed must be the time when it should have come for himself and his old wife. I do not think that he ever looked much to the principle which I had in view. He had no great ideas as to the imbecility and weakness of human life when protracted beyond its fitting limits.

He only felt that it would be good to give up ; and that if he did so, others might be made to do so too. As soon as a residence at the college was completed, I asked him to fill it ; and now he had been living there, he and his wife together, with an attendant, and drawing his salary as curator for the last three years. I thought that it would be the very place for him. He was usually melancholy, disheartened, and impoverished ; but he was always glad to see me, and I was accustomed to go frequently to the college, in order to find a sympathetic soul with whom to converse about the future of the establishment. " Well, Graybody," I said, " I suppose we are nearly ready for the first comer."

"Oh yes ; we're always ready ; but then the first comer is not." I had not said much to him during the latter months as to Crasweller, in particular. His name used formerly to be very ready in all my conversations with Graybody, but of late I had talked to him in a more general tone. "You can't tell me yet when it's to be, Mr President ? We do find it a little dull here."

Now he knew as well as I did the day and the year of Crasweller's birth. I had intended to speak to him about Crasweller, but I wished our friend's name to come first from him. "I suppose it will be some time about mid-winter," I said.

"Oh, I didn't know whether it might not have been postponed "

"How can it be postponed ? As years creep on, you cannot postpone their step. If there might be postponement such as that, I doubt whether we should ever find the time for our inhabitants to come. No, Graybody ; there can be no postponement for the Fixed Period."

"It might have been made sixty-nine or seventy," said he.

"Originally, no doubt. But the wisdom of the Assembly has settled all that. The Assembly has declared that they in Britannula who are left alive at sixty-seven shall on that day be brought into the college. You yourself have, I think, ten years to run, and you will not be much longer left to pass them in solitude."

"It is weary being here all alone, I must confess. Mrs G. says that she could not bear it for another twelve months. The girl we have has given us notice, and she is the ninth within a year. No followers will come after them here, because they say they'll smell the dead bodies."

"Rubbish!" I exclaimed, angrily, "positive rubbish! The actual clay will evaporate into the air, without leaving a trace either for the eye to see or the nose to smell."

"They all say that when you tried the furnaces there was a savour of burnt pork." Now great trouble was taken in that matter of cremation; and having obtained from Europe and the States all the best machinery for the purpose, I had supplied four immense hogs, in order that the system might be fairly tested, and I had fattened them for the purpose, as old men are not unusually very stout. These we consumed in the furnaces all at the same time, and the four bodies had been dissolved into their original atoms without leaving a trace behind them by which their former condition of life might be recognised. But a trap-door in certain of the chimneys had been left open by accident,—either that or by an enemy on purpose, — and undoubtedly some slight flavour of the pig had been allowed to escape. I had been there on the spot, knowing that I could trust only my own senses, and was able to declare that the scent which had escaped was very slight, and by no means disagreeable. And I was able to show that the trap-door had been left open either by chance or by design, —the very trap-door which was intended to prevent any such escape during the moments of full cremation,—so that there need be no fear of a repetition of the accident. I ought, indeed, to have supplied four other hogs, and to have tried the experiment again. But the theme was disagreeable, and I thought that the trial had been so far successful as to make it unnecessary that the expense should be again incurred. "They say that men and women would not have quite the same smell," said he.

"How do they know that?" I exclaimed, in my anger. "How do they know what men and women will smell like? They haven't tried. There won't be any smell at all—not the least; and the smoke will all consume itself, so that even you, living just where you are, will not know when cremation is going on. We might consume all Gladstonopolis, as I hope we shall some day, and not a living soul would know anything about it. But the prejudices of the citizens are ever the stumbling-blocks of civilisation."

"At any rate, Mrs G. tells me that Jemima is going, because none of the young men will come up and see her."

This was another difficulty, but a small one, and I made up my mind that it should be overcome. "The shrubs seem to grow very well," I said, resolved to appear as cheerful as possible.

"They're pretty nearly all alive," said Graybody; "and they do give the place just an appearance like the cemetery at Old Christchurch." He meant the capital in the province of Canterbury.

"In the course of a few years you will be quite—cheerful here."

"I don't know much about that, Mr President. I'm not sure that for myself I want to be cheerful anywhere. If I've only got somebody just to speak to sometimes, that will be quite enough for me. I suppose old Crasweller will be the first?"

"I suppose so."

"It will be a gruesome time when I have to go to bed early, so as not to see the smoke come out of his chimney."

"I tell you there will be nothing of the kind. I don't suppose you will even know when they're going to cremate him."

"He will be the first, Mr President; and no doubt he will be looked closely after. Old Barnes will be here by that time, won't he, sir?"

"Barnes is the second, and he will come just three months before Crasweller's departure. But Tallowax, the grocer in High Street, will be up here by that time. And then they will come so quickly, that we must soon see to get other lodgings finished. Exors, the lawyer, will be the fourth; but he will not come in till a day or two after Crasweller's departure."

"They all will come; won't they, sir?" asked Graybody.

"Will come! Why, they must. It is the law."

"Tallowax swears he'll have himself strapped to his own kitchen table, and defend himself to the last gasp with a carving-knife. Exors says that the law is bad, and you can't touch him. As for Barnes, he has gone out of what little wits he ever had with the fright of it, and people seem to think that you couldn't touch a lunatic."

" Barnes is no more a lunatic than I am."

" I only tell you what folk tell me. I suppose you'll try it on by force, if necessary. You never expected that people would come and deposit themselves of their own accord "

"The National Assembly expects that the citizens of Britannula will obey the law."

" But there was one question I was going to ask, Mr President. Of course I am altogether on your side, and do not wish to raise difficulties. But what shall I do suppose they take to running away after they have been deposited? If old Crasweller goes off in his steam-carriage, how am I to go after him, and whom am I to ask to help to bring him back again?"

I was puzzled, but I did not care to show it.

No doubt a hundred little arrangements would be necessary before the affairs of the institution could be got into a groove so as to run steadily. But our first object must be to deposit Crasweller and Barnes and Tallowax, so that the citizens should be accustomed to the fashion of depositing the aged. There were, as I knew, two or three old women living in various parts of the island, who would, in due course, come in towards the end of Crasweller's year. But it had been rumoured that they had already begun to invent falsehoods as to their age, and I was aware that we might be led astray by them. This I had been prepared to accept as being unavoidable; but now, as the time grew nearer, I could not but see how difficult it would be to enforce the law against well-known men, and how easy to allow the women to escape by the help of falsehood. Exors, the lawyer, would say at once that we did not even attempt to carry out the law; and Barnes, lunatic as he pretended to be, would be very hard to manage. My mind misgave me as I thought of all these obstructions, and I felt that I could so willingly deposit myself at once, and then depart without waiting for my year of probation. But it was necessary that I should show a determined front to old Graybody, and make him feel that I at any rate was determined to remain firm to my purpose. "Mr Crasweller will give you no such trouble as you suggest," said I.

"Perhaps he has come round."

"He is a gentleman whom we have both known intimately for many years, and he has always been a friend to the Fixed Period. I believe that he is so still, although there is some little hitch as to the exact time at which he should be deposited."

"Just twelve months, he says."

"Of course," I replied, "the difference would be sure to be that of one year. He seems to think that there are only nine years between him and me."

"Ten, Mr President; ten.   I know the time well."

"I had always thought so; but I should be willing to abandon a year if I could make things run smooth by doing so.   But all that is a detail with which up here we need not, perhaps, concern ourselves.'

"Only the time is getting very short, Mr President, and my old woman will break down altogether if she's told that she's to live another year all alone.   Crasweller won't be a bit readier next year than he is this; and of course if he is let off, you must let off Barnes and Tallowax.   And there are a lot of old women about who are beginning to tell terrible lies about their ages.   Do think of it all, Mr President."

I never thought of anything else, so full was my mind of the subject.   When I woke in the morning, before I could face the light of day, it was necessary that I should fortify myself with Columbus and Galileo.   I began to fancy, as the danger became nearer and still nearer, that neither of those great men had been surrounded by obstructions such as encompassed me. To plough on across the waves, and either to be drowned or succeed; to tell a new truth about the heavens, and either to perish or become great for ever!—either was within the compass of a man who had only his own life to risk. My life,—how willingly could I run any risk, did but the question arise of risking it! How often I felt, in these days, that there is a fortitude needed by man much greater than that of jeopardising his life! Life! what is it? Here was that poor Crasweller, belying himself and all his convictions just to gain one year more of it, and then when the year was gone he would still have his deposition before him! Is it not so with us all? For me I feel, — have felt for years,—tempted to rush on, and pass through the gates of death. That man should shudder at the thought of it does not appear amiss to me. The unknown future is always awful; and the unknown future of another world, to be approached by so great a change of circumstances, — by the loss of our very flesh and blood and body itself,—has in it something so fearful to the imagination that the man who thinks of it cannot but be struck with horror as he acknowledges that by himself too it has to be encountered. But it has to be encountered; and though the change be awful, it should not therefore, by the sane judgment, be taken as a change necessarily for the worst. Knowing the great goodness of the Almighty, should we not be prepared to accept it as a change probably for the better; as an alteration of our circumstances, by which our condition may be immeasurably improved? Then one is driven back to consider the circumstances by which such change may be effected. To me it seems rational to suppose that as we leave this body so shall we enter that new phase of life in which we are destined to live:—but with all our higher resolves somewhat sharpened, and with our lower passions, alas! made stronger also. That theory by which a human being shall jump at once to a perfection of bliss, or fall to an eternity of evil and misery, has never found credence with me. For myself, I have to say that, while acknowledging my many drawbacks, I have so lived as to endeavour to do good to others, rather than evil, and that therefore I look to my departure from this world with awe indeed, but still with satisfaction. But I cannot look with satisfaction to a condition of life in which, from my own imbecility, I must necessarily retrograde into selfishness. It may be that He who judges of us with a wisdom which I cannot approach, shall take all this into account, and that He shall so mould my future being as to fit it to the best at which I had arrived in this world; still I cannot but fear that a taint of that selfishness which I have hitherto avoided,

but which will come if I allow myself to become old, may remain, and that it will be
better for me that I should go hence while
as yet my own poor wants are not altogether
uppermost in my mind. But then, in arranging this matter, I am arranging it for my
fellow-citizens, and not for myself. I have
to endeavour to think how Crasweller's mind
may be affected rather than my own. He
dreads his departure with a trembling, currish
fear; and I should hardly be doing good to
him were I to force him to depart in a frame
of mind so poor and piteous. But then, again,
neither is it altogether of Crasweller that I
must think,—not of Crasweller or of myself.
How will the coming ages of men be affected
by such a change as I propose, should such
a change become the normal condition of
Death? Can it not be brought about that
men should arrange for their own departure,
so as to fall into no senile weakness, no
slippered selfishness, no ugly whinings of un-

defined want, before they shall go hence, and be no more thought of? These are the ideas that have actuated me, and to them I have been brought by seeing the conduct of those around me. Not for Crasweller, or Barnes, or Tallowax, will this thing be good, — nor for those old women who are already lying about their ages in their cottages,—nor for myself, who am, I know, too apt to boast of myself, that even though old age should come upon me, I may be able to avoid the worst of its effects; but for those untold generations to come, whose lives may be modelled for them under the knowledge that at a certain Fixed Period they shall depart hence with all circumstances of honour and glory.

I was, however, quite aware that it would be useless to spend my energy in dilating on this to Mr Graybody. He simply was willing to shuffle off his mortal coil, because he found it uncomfortable in the wearing. In all likelihood, had his time come as nigh as that of Crasweller, he too, like Crasweller, would impotently implore the grace of another year. He would ape madness like Barnes, or arm himself with a carving-knife like Tallowax, or swear that there was a flaw in the law, as Exors was disposed to do. He too would clamorously swear that he was much younger, as did the old women. Was not the world peopled by Craswellers, Tallowaxes, Exorses, and old women? Had I a right to hope to alter the feelings which nature herself had implanted in the minds of men? But still it might be done by practice,—by practice; if only we could arrive at the time in which practice should have become practice. Then, as I was about to depart from the door of Graybody's house, I whispered to myself again the names of Galileo and Columbus.

"You think that he will come on the thirtieth?" said Graybody, as he took my hand at parting.

"I think," replied I, "that you and I, as loyal citizens of the Republic, are bound to suppose that he will do his duty as a citizen." Then I went, leaving him standing in doubt at his door.

END OF THE FIRST VOLUME.

PRINTED BY WILLIAM BLACKWOOD AND SONS.